THE STORY OF BING & GRØNDAHL CHRISTMAS PLATES

by
Pat Owen

Gifts from
Karen Margreta Imports
Corona del Mar, California

BY THE SAME AUTHOR
The Story of Royal Copenhagen Christmas Plates

TO
Murnie V. ("Buzz") Owen
to whom
this book and this author
are dedicated.

Library of Congress Catalog Card Number: 62-20284.

Typography by Alex Kaye & Associates, Dayton, Ohio.

Printed in the United States of America.

Acknowledgments

This is perhaps the hardest part of any book to write because a book can never be written without the help of many persons. If everyone who helped were thanked individually, this part of the book would become quite lengthy. It is impossible to properly credit all sources deserving of it, but to those who have helped in any way, I wish to extend my sincere thanks.

I am especially indebted to Ole Simonsen, President of the Bing & Grøndahl Porcelain Factory in Copenhagen. Mr. Simonsen has been most helpful and cooperative throughout the preparation of this book. He checked the entire manuscript and gave me many worthwhile suggestions. He provided answers to numerous questions, and gave me much information on the history of the company.

The Biblical quotation on Page 52 is from the *Revised Standard Version of the Bible,* copyright 1946 and 1952 by the Division of Christian Education, National Council of Churches, and used by permission.

I wish to thank *Hobbies* Magazine for permitting me to use material from an article I did for that magazine on the history of the Bing & Grøndahl Porcelain Factory.

I am most grateful to my husband "Buzz" for his help. He has patiently gone through the entire manuscript with me page by page, acting as a critic, and thereby causing me to rewrite and rewrite. I am sure this is a better book because of his criticism and helpful suggestions.

I would certainly be amiss if I did not send a word of

thanks to my good friend Bent Møller of Copenhagen, who first introduced me to the lovely Bing & Grøndahl Christmas Plates about twelve years ago. That introduction was one that led me not only into the hobby of collecting Christmas Plates, but also into the business of importing and selling them. Through this business I have met Christmas Plate collectors all over the country who have often asked for more information about the plates. This interest has prompted me to do research on the subject for the last eleven years. The result is this book and my hope is that it will help collectors to better appreciate and enjoy their lovely Christmas Plates.

Pat Owen
(Mrs. M. V. Owen)

Dayton, Ohio
August, 1962

Foreword

When my grandfather, the late Harald Bing, in 1895 conceived the idea of the world's first Christmas Plate he wanted not only to create a Christmas greeting or gift of particular quality and beauty, but also a series of Danish sceneries, historic buildings, etc., that would appeal to collectors all over the world and at the same time make them interested in his beloved mother country.

How well the idea caught on and spread like wildfire is witnessed by the present book, issued in the year of our sixty-eighth (1962) Christmas Plate. I would like to express my appreciation of Pat Owen's work, which should prove a useful guide to all collectors while at the same time providing them with interesting glimpses into the history and customs of the world's oldest kingdom, Denmark.

Ole Simonsen,
President,
Bing & Grøndahl
Porcelain Factory

Contents

For information as to how this book may be kept up-to-date, consult the store from which you purchased it, or write the publisher:

Viking Import House,
1975 Burnham Lane,
Dayton, Ohio 45429

(The photograph opposite this page is of a painting of the Bing & Grøndahl Porcelain Factory in the middle 1850's.)

9

The Legend Of Christmas Plates

Many, many years ago the wealthy people of Europe started a Christmas custom of giving to each of their servants a platter heaped with fruit, cookies, candies and other good things to eat. At first the platter was probably a crude thing of wood, and very little thought was given to it. The rich focused their attention on the contents of the tray, hoping to bring a little cheer into the lives of the recipients by giving them especially good things to eat around the holiday season.

The servants looked forward each Christmas to receiving their gifts. Since these people had few things in their homes which were not utilitarian, perhaps it was only natural that they began hanging the platters on their walls after the food was eaten. They referred to these platters as their "Christmas Plates."

Later the servants of one family started showing their Christmas Plates to the servants of other households. When the employers realized that there was rivalry among the servants of the various households regarding who received the most beautiful plates, they began giving more consideration to the platter itself. Eventually beautiful platters were made of many materials, such as metal, wood and pottery. They were sometimes elaborately carved or decoratively painted. In fact, the wealthy, in an effort to outdo each other, commenced devoting more attention to the plate itself than to its contents. Later they started dating each platter so that it would be easy to see which year each had been given. Thus began the custom of making and collecting Christmas Plates.

10

A Brief History Of Bing & Grøndahl
THE NATIONAL FACTORY OF PORCELAIN

Bing & Grøndahl was established in 1853 when Copenhagen was still a small town. The factory was situated out in the country a little west of town and, as shown by the painting on page 8, was surrounded by green fields and trees. Some of the original buildings are still in use today, but they are now completely surrounded by the city of Copenhagen.

Frederik Vilhelm Grøndahl, a young sculptor, left the employ of The Royal Copenhagen Porcelain Manufactory when that company refused to go along with his suggestion that the figurines of the famous sculptor Thorvaldsen be copied in "biscuit" (unglazed) porcelain. Having considerably more ambition than money, Grøndahl took his ideas to M. H. and J. H. Bing, prosperous businessmen who owned a store which sold stationery, books and objects of art. Combining the capital and business acumen of the Bing brothers with the artistic ideas of Grøndahl, the Bing & Grøndahl Porcelain Factory became a reality.

Since Denmark is practically void of natural resources, it was necessary from the beginning for the company to import the three main ingredients of porcelain (quartz, feldspar and kaolin), as well as the coloring and firing materials.

Unfortunately, Grøndahl died about a year and a half after the company was started. For several years the Bing brothers struggled to improve their products, succeeding only after skilled craftsmen were brought in from abroad. Gradually the company gained recognition in Denmark and, eventually, demand for its products spread to other countries.

About 1886 Bing & Grøndahl learned the secrets of underglaze painting. Before that time the company had made many beautiful objects such as dinnerware, vases and figurines, but they had always been made in either "biscuit" or overglaze porcelain. In 1889 Bing & Grøndahl created quite a stir in the artistic world by showing at the Paris World Fair its new stately "Heron" Service designed by Pietro Krohn, and executed in the medium of underglaze painting.

The company was incorporated in 1895 with the Bing family retaining the controlling interest. In the same year Harald Bing, then head of the company, conceived the idea of issuing an annual Christmas Plate, using the new underglaze technique. This was the first time in history that Christmas Plates had been produced commercially. The first plate was placed on the market shortly before Christmas that year and bore the inscription *Jule Aften 1895* (Christmas Eve 1895). Each year since, a seven-inch blue and white plate has been made. Orders from the company's distributors for the Christmas Plates are accepted only through June 30 of each year. After Christmas all molds are destroyed so as to prevent any reproduction later, thus enhancing the value to collectors.

In 1915 Bing & Grøndahl brought out a Jubilee Plate in commemoration of the first Christmas Plate. The motif of one of the Christmas Plates was chosen to be used on this nine-inch plate and the inscription was *1895 Jule Aften 1915*. The coloring was the same blue and white as the Christmas Plates. Every fifth year since 1915 a new Jubilee Plate has been issued.

The company also produced a series of blue and white *Paaske* (Easter) Plaques starting with the year 1910 and continuing through 1935.

12

During the next few decades following the introduction of underglaze porcelain, the company had several great artists in its employ, including J. F. Willusmen, Effie Hegermann-Lindencrone, Fanny Garde, Hans Tegner, Kai Nielsen and Jean Gauguin. During this period Bing & Grøndahl received the *Grand Prix* several times, thereby winning wide acclaim.

Bing & Grøndahl exhibited stoneware for the first time in 1914. Large scale production in this field, however, has never been attempted. Instead, all efforts have been concentrated on producing a series of individual items, many of which have been acquired by museums and prominent private collectors. Bing & Grøndahl started making the so-called "soft porcelain" in 1925.

The company erected a second factory in 1949 which is devoted exclusively to manufacturing dinnerware. Bing & Grøndahl also operates a retail outlet in the heart of the Copenhagen shopping district.

Throughout its more than one hundred years the management of the company has remained in the hands of the same family. The President, Ole Simonsen, is descended from one of the Bing founders. Today the company employs approximately twelve hundred persons and in many cases, one generation has succeeded another.

Bing & Grøndahl has, in the course of the years, achieved the honor of being appointed to the Royal Courts of Denmark, Sweden and Great Britain. In many of the world's noted museums, including the Metropolitan Museum of Art in New York, can be found pieces made by the company. Every piece made by Bing & Grøndahl is signed with either the artist's name or initial. Truly it can now be said that pieces with the trademark of the Three Towers can be found in every land where gracious living is prized.

CHRISTMAS PLATES IN THE MAKING

A. The Christmas Plate is shaped and molded. Each mold can be utilized only 20 to 25 times. After that a new mold must be used

B. Each molded Christmas Plate is carefully examined for any imperfections. Only perfect specimens are allowed to continue the

C. After the first firing (for 20 hours), the Christmas Plate is hand-painted.

F. The Christmas Plates are meticulously inspected prior to shipment.

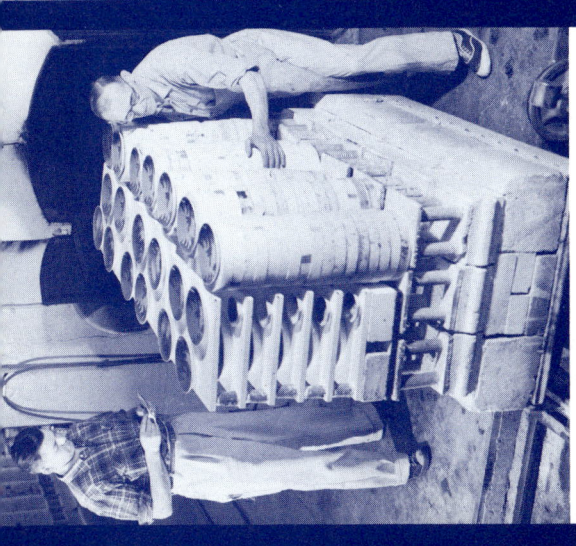

E. The Plates are carefully removed from the oven where they have been fired at 2700 to 2800 degrees for a period of 28 to 30 hours.

D. The Christmas Plate is dipped in glaze before the final firing.

Painstaking craftsmanship and uncompromising quality are the foundations for Bing & Grøndahl's international renown.

The Story Of The Danish Flag

Denmark's flag is the oldest on earth, dating back to June 15, 1219, and the story of its origin is most unusual.

Valdemar the Victorious, King of Denmark from 1202-1241, extended Denmark's domain by conquering Esthonia. During one of the major battles of this war, the Danes found themselves greatly outnumbered and almost completely surrounded. As they retreated, the archbishop and many of the soldiers knelt to pray. The legend goes that as they prayed to God for guidance, a red banner with a white cross in it came floating gently down through the clouds. A heavenly voice was heard to say that the Danes should take this banner and return to battle. This they did and the Esthonians were quickly conquered.

This miraculous banner was known as *Dannebrog* (Danes' Cloth). For three hundred years the original banner was carried in all wars. It eventually disappeared during a battle against Germany, but replicas of the original are still used for the Danish flag today.

The Danish people are proud of their flag and fly it often. They display it not only on holidays and the King's birthday, but also on their own, their children's, their grandchildren's and their grandparents' birthdays and silver-wedding anniversaries. They also use small flags to help decorate their Christmas trees.

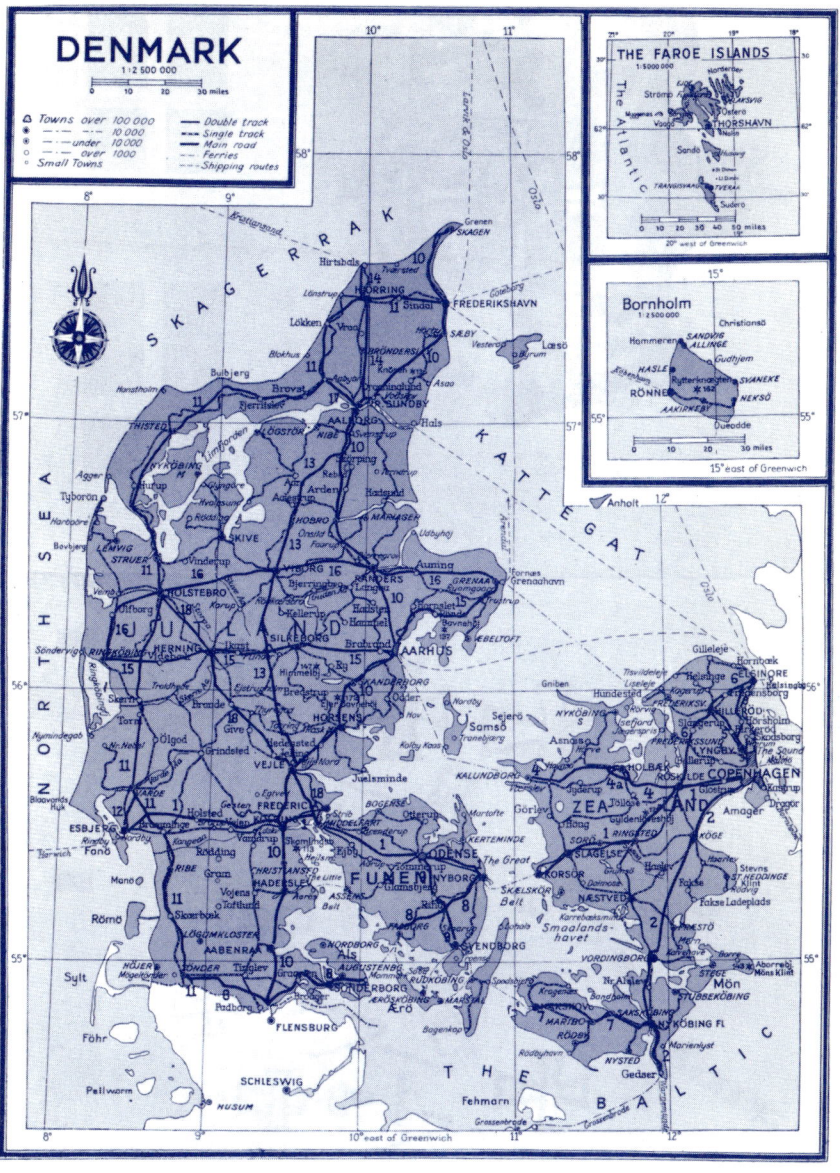

DENMARK

1:2 500 000

△ Towns over 100 000	——— Double track
◉ —·—·— 10 000	——— Single track
◉ —·—·— under 10 000	——— Main road
○ —·—·— over 1 000	——— Ferries
○ Small Towns	——— Shipping routes

THE FAROE ISLANDS
1:5000 000

20° west of Greenwich

Bornholm
1:2 500 000

15° east of Greenwich

17

List of Danish Kings

Gorm the Old	900-940	Valdemar the Great	1157-1182
Harald Bluetooth	940-985	Canute	1182-1202
Sweyn Forkbeard	985-1014	Valdemar the Victorious	1202-1241
Harald Sweynson	1014-1018	Erik IV Ploughpenny	1241-1250
Canute the Great	1018-1035	Abel	1250-1252
Hardicanute	1035-1042	Christopher I	1252-1259
Magnus the Good	1042-1047	Erik V Klipping	1259-1286
Sweyn Estrithson	1047-1076	Erik VI Menved	1286-1320
Harald Hen	1076-1080	Christopher II	1320-1326
Canute the Holy	1080-1086	Valdemar Eriksson	1326-1330
Olaf Hunger	1086-1095	Christopher II	1330-1332
Erik the Evergood	1095-1103	Period of strife (no king)	1332-1340
Niels	1104-1134	Valdemar IV Atterdag	1340-1376
Erik II Emune	1134-1137	Oluf	1376-1387
Erik III Lamm	1137-1146	Queen Margaret	1387-1412
Sweyn, Canute and		Erik of Pomerania	1412-1439
Valdemar	1146-1157	Christopher of Bavaria	1439-1448

The Oldenburg Dynasty
(with the line of Glucksborg)

Christian I	1448-1481	Christian VI	1730-1746
Hans	1481-1513	Frederik V	1746-1766
Christian II	1513-1523	Christian VII	1766-1808
Frederik I	1523-1533	Frederik VI	1808-1839
Christian III	1534-1559	Christian VIII	1839-1848
Frederik II	1559-1588	Frederik VII	1848-1863
Christian IV	1588-1648	Christian IX	1863-1906
Frederik III	1648-1670	Frederik VIII	1906-1912
Christian V	1670-1699	Christian X	1912-1947
Frederik IV	1699-1730	Frederik IX	1947-

Behind the Frozen Window
by
F. A. Hallin

1895

What motif could be more appropriate for the very first Christmas Plate than the skyline of that city so often referred to as the "City of Beautiful Spires"?

Through the frosted windowpane of the Frederiksberg Castle on Frederiksberg Hill the skyline of Copenhagen is seen on a cold, clear night. Frederik IV built the castle in 1704 as a summer residence. Today it is used as a school for training military officers.

Along the skyline may be recognized, among other buildings, the contours of such famous structures as the Marble Church, the Round Tower with the Trinitatis Church, the St. Nicolai Church tower (the devastated spire was not reconstructed until 1909-1911), the Royal Stock Exchange and the Church of Our Lady (the Copenhagen Cathedral). The history of each of these buildings is closely interwoven with that of Copenhagen. The city was founded by Bishop Absalon in 1167 and called *Castrum de Hafn* (Merchant's Haven). While Copenhagen was still a small fishing village Absalon built a fortified castle with three towers to defend it. That is the reason why the City of Copenhagen chose the Three Towers for its coat of arms, and also why Bing & Grøndahl selected the same Three Towers for its trademark.

Copenhagen boasts many fine old buildings but the ones outlined on this plate are still among those most admired.

Not realizing how much the world would cherish these Christmas Plates, Bing & Grøndahl conservatively made only four hundred. Today this plate is much sought after by collectors and commands a very high price.

New Moon Over Snow-Covered Trees
by
F. A. Hallin

1896

Today there is not a single acre of virgin forest left in Denmark. In the eighteenth century when the wooded areas of the country had diminished until they represented only four percent of the total, the government began to recognize the threatening shortage of wood. It was then that strict laws were enacted to preserve Denmark's forests. Had it not been for these laws, Denmark would probably be without forests today.

The government has made it imperative that new trees be planted when an old stand is cut. It has also imported conifers and broadleaf trees from all over the world, and years of experimentation have determined the trees best suited to Denmark's soil and climate.

Experiments with many foreign species of trees resulted in a keen interest in controlled harvesting of forest tree seeds. There have been established in recent years special tree breeding nurseries to raise seeds from selected trees under controlled pollination. Denmark is also known for its principles of selective thinning of forests. These principles, developed during the last century, are now followed in all European countries.

Today about 1,800,000 acres, about ten and two-tenths percent of Denmark's total area, are in forests. About one-fourth of the wooded area is owned by the government. Spruce and fir predominate in Jutland, though beech can also be found there in abundance. Funen, often called Denmark's garden, has many fruit trees, willows and poplars. Beech and oak are the most common trees of Zealand.

Christmas Meal of the Sparrows
by
F. A. Hallin

1897

At Christmas, perhaps more than at any other time, we think of the animals and birds of the fields and forests. This plate portrays the artist's conception of sparrows having their Christmas meal. The painting also depicts an old method of twisting wheat stalks into a rope to bind a shock.

It is an ancient Scandinavian custom that the farmers put aside one sheaf of wheat from the harvest which they tie to a pole at Christmas to be a feast for the birds. The city people also remember their feathered friends, especially at Christmas, by clearing the snow from the window ledge and leaving bread crumbs for them.

Before 1880 the Danish farmers devoted almost all their land to raising grain, particularly wheat, which was exported to European countries, principally England. Then in the late 1870's and early 1880's the vast new grain fields of North America began to provide competition. Grain dropped to one-half its former price. The Danish farmers soon realized it would be necessary to revolutionize their farming system if they were to survive. Within ten years they were concentrating on the raising of hogs, cows and chickens. Today Denmark is known for her exports of butter, bacon and eggs. Grain, though, is still grown in fairly large quantities. The progressive Danish farmer, through his use of imported fertilizers and much hard work, has been able to increase his yield per acre two to three times that of the average farmer in the United States. Nevertheless, the Danish farmers do not now raise enough grain to meet the needs of the country, and every year much grain is imported.

24

Christmas Roses and Christmas Star
by
Fanny Garde

1898

Perhaps the artist who made the original painting of this Christmas Plate received his inspiration from the legend of the Christmas rose. According to the legend a little girl had accompanied her father to the fields on that night when the angel appeared before the shepherds telling them that a Savior had been born in Bethlehem (see story for 1911 plate). The older shepherds went at once to find the newborn babe, and the little girl followed them. When they arrived at the stable, the little girl watched as the wise men presented their fine gifts, and the shepherds gave their humble gifts to the Christ Child. She cried softly because she had nothing at all to give. She longed for anything — even a flower — but, alas, there were no blooming flowers. Then the little girl gave the only gift she could — she offered up a prayer that God would bless the Mother and Child. Suddenly as she prayed, roses appeared where her tears had fallen. She gathered them quickly and gave them to the Christ Child who immediately turned his attention from the gems and gold of the wise men to the lovely roses. Then he smiled at the little girl who had given him first of all the gift of love and, secondly, the first Christmas roses.

Another legend claims that what we call Christmas roses bloomed first in the garden of Eden where they were known as Roses of Affection.

The U. S. Department of Agriculture believes that the Christmas rose is a native of Great Britain. In any event, the plant retains the habit of blooming around Christmas time. Frost and snow do not seemingly deter the blooming. The blossoms are usually white but turn a pale pink as they begin to fade.

26

The Crows Enjoying Christmas
by
Dahl Jensen

1899

This plate shows two crows sitting on a snow-covered tree branch on Christmas Eve. Perhaps they are aware that somehow the world is a little different on this one night of the year. Surely they have noticed and taken advantage of the sheaves of wheat put out on poles by the Danish farmers at Christmas time. Crows are quite numerous in Denmark and because they are often a nuisance, they are sometimes killed by the farmers.

Other birds found in Denmark's wooded areas include the sparrow hawk, falcon, buzzard, jay, thrush and woodpecker. Among the garden visitors are the sparrow, tomtit, finch, starling, nightingale and pigeon. Near the lakes and streams can be found the wild duck, red-breasted merganser, coot, grebe, teal and reed warbler. The oyster-catcher, dunlin, lapwing, curlew, ringer plover, gull and tern live on the beaches.

The scene on this plate is from the island of Als in Southern Jutland. The church in the background is the old Notmark Church which was constructed in Romanesque style hundreds of years ago of granite boulders and consecrated to Our Lady. In the Middle Ages the choir was enlarged and a tower added. The gables of this tower were placed north and south as was the custom on the island of Funen.

Not far from the Notmark Church is Dybbøl Mill, shown on the 1947 Christmas plate.

The island of Als is also famous for its great number of ancient burial places. In the state-owned forest of Bloomeskol is found one of Denmark's best preserved cairns, dating back about four thousand years.

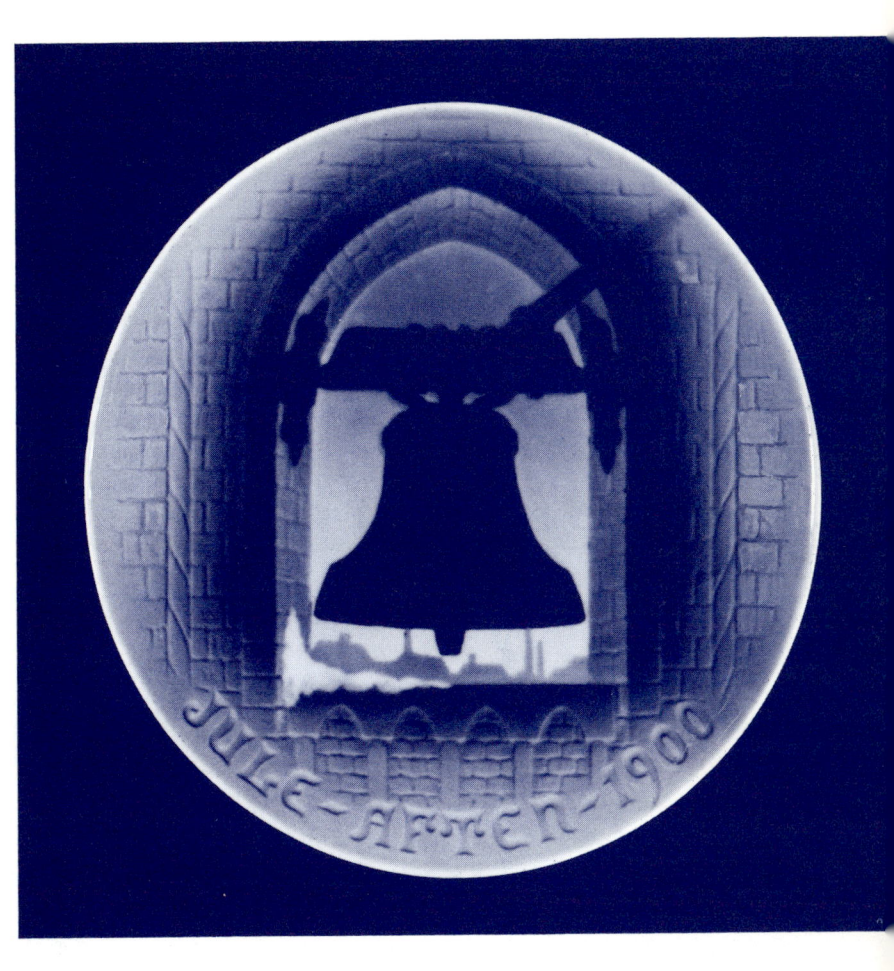

Church Bells Chiming in Christmas
by
Dahl Jensen

1900

This beautiful church bell is located in the church tower of the *Syv* (Seven) Church in the neighborhood of Roskilde, eighteen miles west of Copenhagen. The bell was cast in 1515 by one of the finest bell founders who ever worked in Denmark, Johannes Fastenove of the Netherlands.

The town of Roskilde was founded by King Roar about A.D. 500 and was the capital of Denmark until 1416. It was one of the richest towns in Denmark from the twelfth through the fourteenth century. It was the seat of the bishops who owned not only the great Roskilde Cathedral but also much of Copenhagen. The Reformation changed all this and Roskilde lost its former importance.

The Roskilde Cathedral was consecrated in 1084. Today it is Denmark's Westminister Abbey as thirty-six kings and queens and more than one hundred persons of royal blood have been buried there. Harald Bluetooth was the first king laid to rest there, and Christian X who died in 1947 was the last.

In Danish the word *Roskilde* means *Roar's Spring,* and there are a number of springs in the town and the surrounding territory. One of the most important springs is the *Maglekilde* which gives off one hundred gallons of water per minute.

In the Town Hall Square of Roskilde is a sculpture of the founder, King Roar, and his brother, Helge. The inscription on the pedestal when translated is:

> *At the springs of Lejre*
> *With pride I'll wear my crown,*
> *Do justice to any man in my realm*
> *And here I'll build my town.*

The Three Wise Men from the East
by
S. Sabra

This plate could easily be an illustration for the story of the wise men as told in Matthew 2:1-11 of the Bible.

The Bible does not give the number of wise men, but Christian tradition has always set the number at three, and even given them names of Melchior, Caspar and Balthasar. Perhaps tradition has held that there were three wise men because three gifts were presented to Jesus – gold, frankincense and myrrh. A legend that was circulating during the Middle Ages in Persia, believed to have been the home of the Magi, gave a specific purpose for three gifts. According to the legend three wise men once went on a long journey to visit a newborn prophet. They wished to find out whether the baby would become a god, an earthly king or a physician, and they carried gold, frankincense and myrrh to determine this. The wise men reasoned that if the baby took the incense first he would be a god. If he should take the gold first, he would then be an earthly king. To take the myrrh first would indicate that he would become a physician.

In paintings and in dramas the wise men have most often been depicted as presenting their gifts to the infant Jesus in the manger. Yet the Bible definitely states that the wise men entered a house to see the child. It is believed that the holy family moved from the stable to a house on the eastern slopes of the town before the wise men arrived. Today there is a Franciscan chapel where the house is supposed to have been.

When Marco Polo visited Persia in the thirteenth century he made diligent inquiries about the Magi. He was told they had returned to their home city of Saba and later were buried in a beautiful tomb.

Interior of a Gothic Church
by
Dahl Jensen

1902

The artist of this Christmas Plate portrayed his impression of a Lutheran Church at Christmas, with candlelight radiating a sensation of peace in the lofty Gothic style sanctuary.

Christianity first gained a foothold in Denmark about the tenth century. Until about 1536 Catholicism reigned supreme in Denmark. Then came the Reformation and the Lutheran principles took root and still govern the church. According to the Danish Constitution the Lutheran Church is the National Church of Denmark, and as such is supported by the State. The confessional scriptures of the National Church are the Old and New Testaments, the three symbols of the primitive church (the Creed, the Nicene and the Athanasian symbols), the original unaltered Augsburg Declaration of Faith of 1530, and Luther's Little Catechism.

Laws on matters pertaining to the church are enacted by the King and the *Folketing* (Danish Parliament) like other legislation. The National Church is administered by the Ministry of Ecclesiastical Affairs. The question of giving the National Church its own Constitution has often been discussed, but the proposal has never been carried out. The country is divided into nine *stifts* (dioceses), each with its own bishop and archdeacon (bishop's assistant). Each diocese is subdivided into parishes, each with a church and a minister. There are about 1700 parishes in Denmark today. All ministers, with very few exceptions, hold a theological degree. In 1957 women were admitted to holy orders in the National Church.

Happy Expectation of the Children
by
Margrethe Hyldahl

1903

Children in Denmark are the same as they are everywhere else – for weeks before Christmas, they eagerly anticipate the season. During December evenings they make decorations for the Christmas tree. They shop for gifts and try to keep what they bought a secret until Christmas Eve. Christmas Eve is the big time for celebrating the holiday in Denmark. It is on this evening that the big Christmas dinner is eaten. Perhaps the three children shown on this plate are thinking of that delicious Christmas Eve dinner and the exciting things that follow the dinner (see story for 1909 plate).

The traditional Christmas dinner in Denmark always begins with everyone eating rice porridge. There is a huge bowl of porridge, usually sprinkled with cinnamon and with a piece of butter in the center. Sometimes, though, it is served with fruit juice or even sweetened beer over it. Somewhere in the porridge is an almond, and everyone must eat porridge until it is found. The person who finds the almond gets a special present called the almond present. In households with several children, it sometimes happens that each child finds an almond, and gets a special present. But whether there are children or not, it wouldn't be a Danish Christmas dinner without everyone first eating rice porridge.

Then comes the main course. The traditional dinner is truly a feast, and always includes roast goose stuffed with apples and prunes, small caramel-browned potatoes and red cabbage. While Americans like their fruitcake and the English like their plum pudding, the Danes prefer to end their Christmas dinner with apple cake (layers of bread crumbs, apple sauce and jam) topped with whipped cream.

36

View of Copenhagen from the Frederiksberg Hill
by
Cathinka Olsen

1904

This plate shows essentially the same view as the 1895 Christmas Plate. Here, though, the skyline of Copenhagen is being observed from the outside of Frederiksberg Castle instead of behind the frosted window. The time is nine years later and the skyline is a little changed. The greatest difference is probably the Town Hall of Copenhagen, outlined on the right of the plate. The Town Hall, depicted more clearly on the 1930 plate, was still under construction in 1904 and was officially inaugurated in 1905.

Frederiksberg is a municipality adjoining Copenhagen to the southwest. The Frederiksberg Hill formerly offered a perfect view of Copenhagen as can be seen from the painting on this plate. On top of the hill is the main entrance of the Copenhagen Zoological Gardens, founded in 1859 and considered to be the finest and oldest in all Scandinavia. Here on twenty acres of ground may be found hundreds of species of mammals, birds, reptiles, amphibians, fish and invertebrates.

The Frederiksberg Park, containing many stately old trees and picturesque canals, is the largest and most pleasing of the royal gardens in the area of Copenhagen. Beautiful Chinese pavilions have been built on some of the islets. The people of Frederiksberg and Copenhagen once promenaded in the park dressed in their Sunday best and sat on the *Sladrebaenke* (gossip benches) in front of the statue of Frederik VI who was very popular in his time. He often sailed in a barge on the canals wearing an admiral's uniform, while accepting the hearty and respectful greetings of his faithful subjects.

38

Anxiety of the Coming Christmas Night
by
Dahl Jensen

1905

The graceful deer standing under a snow laden tree is in the Klampenborg Deer Park *(Dyrehaven)*. The artist has tried to let it symbolize the anxiety and the feeling of holiness that comes with Christmas. The deer is all alone, and in its solitude it senses that something unusual, something sacred has happened: Christmas has come.

In 1670 Christian V enclosed two thousand acres a few miles north of Copenhagen for hunting purposes. Today the park is perhaps the most popular excursion place of the Copenhageners. Here herds of deer with majestic stags pasture peacefully and provide an enchanting view, especially when seen against the background of the *Eremitage* Castle (shown on the 1923 plate). The deer are seemingly unaware that man is ever an enemy of their kind.

In the park may be found some of the most beautiful woods in all Denmark. Tall birches are the most numerous but oak and fir are also found in great numbers. The deer have completely gnawed away the undergrowth, giving the wooded area a character of its own.

In the southern part of the Deer Park is *Bakken,* the largest amusement park in Northern Europe. In addition to the usual shooting tents, wheels of fortune and various rides normally associated with amusement parks, here are also found beer gardens, restaurants, a dancing pavilion and an open-air theater where performances are sometimes given by members of the Royal Theater of Copenhagen. The taxes levied by the State on the income from the amusement park are used for the upkeep of the forest and to feed the deer in the winter.

40

Sleighing to Church on Christmas Eve
by
Dahl Jensen

1906

This Christmas Plate pictures a farmer and his daughter on their way to church by sleigh. Formerly sleighs were very much in use in the remote parts of Denmark, but today better roads and the introduction of the automobile and other modes of transportation have made the sleigh obsolete.

The church shown on this plate is the Faarevejle Church in the northwestern part of Zealand. This typical village church has become famous because it contains a glass-topped casket that holds the remarkably well-preserved body of the Earl of Bothwell.

Mary, Queen of Scots, in 1565 married her cousin Henry Stuart, or Lord Darnley. Soon thereafter James Hepburn, Earl of Bothwell, fell in love with Mary. In 1567 Lord Darnley was murdered and the Earl of Bothwell was accused of having had something to do with the murder. However, he was acquitted after a trial. Bothwell then kidnapped Mary and made her his wife. The Scots were not pleased about this turn of events and Mary was imprisoned, while Bothwell fled the country. First he went to the Orkney Islands, of which Mary had made him the Duke, and later to Norway where he was captured. He was confined to Malmø Castle in Southern Sweden. The marriage was later dissolved by the Pope. In 1573 Bothwell was transferred to Dragsholm Castle where he was imprisoned until he died five years later completely insane. The body of Bothwell was disinterred about a hundred years ago and found to be in a fine state of preservation. It was placed in a glass-topped casket in nearby Faarevejle Church.

The Dragsholm Castle was long used as a prison, but was blown up by the Swedes in 1659. It was restored about forty years later. Today it is used as a hotel.

The Little Match Girl
by
E. Plockross

1907

This Christmas Plate illustrates one of Hans Christian Andersen's best known fairy tales, "The Little Match Girl". The story was first printed in Copenhagen in 1846 in *Dansk Folkekalender.* Andersen wrote the following about the story: " 'The Little Match Girl' was written at the Castle of Graasten, where I stopped for a few days on a journey abroad, and where I received a letter from the publisher, Mr. Flinch, asking me to write a story for the almanac, to accompany one of three pictures enclosed. The picture I chose was that of a poor little girl with a bundle of matches." The picture referred to by Andersen was a drawing by the Danish painter, J. T. Lundbye (1818-1848).

The story took place on a bitterly cold New Year's Eve. The little match girl was afraid to go home because she had not sold even a penny's worth of matches all day, and she knew her father would beat her. As she sat forlornly on the steps of a house she decided to try to warm herself by lighting one match. The glow of the match made her imagine she was warming herself by a warm stove. The illusion lasted only as long as the match burned. The second match caused her to think there was a delicious roast goose in front of her. With the third match she thought she saw a beautiful Christmas tree. While burning the fourth match, the little girl saw her grandmother, the only person who had ever loved her and who was now dead. In an effort to keep the image of her grandmother with her, she quickly struck match after match. She begged her grandmother to take her along to the place where the grandmother went after each match burned.

The next morning the little match girl was found on the steps, frozen to death with a smile on her face.

44

St. Petri Church of Copenhagen
by
Povl Jørgensen

1908

Copenhagen has many fine old buildings, but St. Petri Church is considered by many to be one of the most beautiful. Certainly it is one of the oldest churches in the city, with records dating back to 1304. It was devastated by fire in 1386 and again in 1728. Damage was once again inflicted in 1807 by Nelson's bombardment. Each time the building was restored.

From 1450 until the Reformation, St. Petri (St. Peter's) was a parish church. Then for several years it was used as a cannon and bell foundry. In 1574 it was adopted by the Germans living in the city and since that time has been known as the German church of Copenhagen. In its present form the church dates back to 1816.

The attractive copper steeple shown on this Christmas Plate was erected during 1756-1757. Inside the church are two silver candelabra given by Queen Sofie Magdalene in 1731. Several monuments may be found in the surrounding gardens.

Diagonally across the street from St. Petri is another famous old church, the Church of Our Lady, which has served as Copenhagen's cathedral since 1924. Nelson's bombardment destroyed the spire of this church and it was never rebuilt. It was replaced by the cross seen today. The facade has six tall columns flanked by bronze statues of Moses and David. Inside the church may be found Thorvaldsen's famous marble figures of "Christ and the Apostles". A soft light glows behind the figure of Christ, showing the carved inscription *"Kommer Til Mig"* ("Come Unto Me"). It was here that many of the medieval kings were crowned, and since 1537 all the bishops, the chief dignitaries of the church, have been consecrated here.

Happiness over the Yule Tree
by
Aarestrup

1909

After the Danish Christmas Eve dinner (see story for 1903 plate) is over and the dishes are finished, mother and father disappear for a few minutes. Expectations are high at this point because everyone knows that they are in the living room lighting the candles on the Christmas tree. Mother and father then open the door with a smile, and everyone rushes to see the beautiful tree. The children have not been allowed to see the tree until this moment, so it is small wonder that the little boy on this Christmas Plate seems to be enthralled. The tree is radiant with candles, tinsel, hearts, baskets filled with sweets, flags, and at the top is a silver star! Around the foot of the tree are all the gaily wrapped gifts.

Before any gift exchanging takes place, it is the custom that all join hands and dance around the tree, singing some of the old Danish Christmas songs. One hymn they always sing is *"Stille Nat"* ("Silent Night"). "Merry Christmas, Lovely Christmas" to the tune of "Holy Night" is also a favorite. Although this singing is definitely part of Christmas in Denmark, Christmas caroling where the singers travel from house to house is never done.

After several songs it is time for what the children have long and eagerly awaited – the gift exchange. On Christmas Eve the children are allowed to "stay up late". When they are finally tucked in for the night with their Christmas gifts stacked at the foot of the bed, they are transported into a world of pleasant dreams.

Christmas Day is normally kept rather quietly. The family generally stays home, and the children play with the toys received the night before.

The Old Organist
by
C. Ersgaard

1910

Practically all Danish churches have an organ and some of the players are internationally known musicians. The organ shown on this Christmas Plate is probably in a medieval church. The dress of the organist is also indicative of the Middle Ages.

Organs go far back into history. It is known they were fully developed at the time of Christ. Hero of Alexandria described an organ in his "Pneumatica" about 100 B.C. Tertullian mentioned a certain Ctesibus as the inventor of the organ, and Archimed as the man who put the finishing touch to it. According to the Spanish Bishop Julianus (about A.D. 450) the organ was first found in Europe in the Spanish churches. It was first heard of in France in A.D. 757 when Emperor Pipin the Little is said to have received an organ as a gift from the Byzantine emperor.

Organs were installed in Denmark during the period of Catholicism. Even today the art of organ building is at a high level in Denmark. In 1961 the organ of the Swedish town *Kristianstad* (named after its founder, Christian IV of Denmark) was rebuilt by a Danish organ builder in its original style.

The design of the beautiful Grundtvig Church in the northwestern part of Copenhagen was inspired by the symmetry of a church organ and the simplicity of the Danish village churches. It is considered one of the world's masterpieces of contemporary religious architecture.

The Danes have always been fond of music, and most homes have some sort of musical instrument. The people of Copenhagen can hear good orchestras at reasonable prices. Foreign operas are rendered in Danish at the Royal Theater.

First It Was Sung by the Angels to the
Shepherds in the Field
by
H. Moltke

1911

This plate depicts the angel appearing before the shepherds at the time of the birth of Christ. Many historians believe that Christ was born in the springtime because the shepherds were watching their flock by night, which they did not ordinarily do except during the season when the lambs were born.

"*And in that region there were shepherds out in the field, keeping watch over their flock by night. And an angel of the Lord appeared to them, and the glory of the Lord shone around them, and they were filled with fear. And the angel said to them, 'Be not afraid; for behold, I bring you good news of a great joy which will come to all the people; for to you is born this day in the city of David a Savior, who is Christ the Lord. And this will be a sign for you: you will find a babe wrapped in swaddling cloths and lying in a manger.' And suddenly there was with the angel a multitude of the heavenly host praising God and saying, 'Glory to God in the highest, and on earth peace among men with whom he is pleased!'*

"*When the angels went away from them into heaven, the shepherds said to one another, 'Let us go over to Bethlehem and see this thing that has happened, which the Lord has made known to us.' And they went with haste, and found Mary and Joseph, and the babe lying in a manger. And when they saw it they made known the saying which had been told them concerning this child; and all who heard it wondered at what the shepherds told them. But Mary kept all these things, pondering them in her heart. And the shepherds returned, glorifying and praising God for all they had heard and seen, as it had been told them.*" (Luke 2:8-20)

Going to Church on Christmas Eve
by
Einar Hansen

1912

The parishioners in this scene are entering Ejby Church for the Christmas Eve service. The town of Ejby is located southwest of Copenhagen and a little northwest of Køge. The church, originally known as Munke-Ejby, was taken over by the Crown after the Reformation. In 1604 it was given to Henrik Gjøe and among the subsequent owners were Corfitz Ulfeldt and Lenora Christina. It was taken from this couple, along with all their other possessions when Ulfeldt was convicted of high treason. Lenora Christina, daughter of Christian IV, spent twenty-two years of her life in prison because of her marriage to Ulfeldt at the age of fifteen. Copenhagen erected a Pillar of Shame *(Skamstøtte)* to Ulfeldt, the most notorious and most hated traitor in Danish history, and the *Skamstøtte* may still be seen in the National Museum.

The Ejby Church is just one of several typical Danish village churches depicted on the Christmas Plates. The pride of the Danish people for their village churches is justified as ninety percent of their churches are over seven hundred years old. During the twelfth and thirteenth centuries there were some seventeen to eighteen hundred churches erected, many of which are still in use.

Up to the middle of the nineteenth century membership in the Lutheran Church was compulsory for Danish subjects. Catholics, Reformists and Jews had residential rights in certain towns. The Constitutional Act of 1849 introduced full religious freedom. Compulsory baptism was later abolished, and civil forms of marriage and burial allowed. Today only the King must profess the faith. The people are free to worship as they choose, provided it is not contrary to public morality and good order.

Bringing Home the Yule Tree
by
Th. Larsen

1913

Conifers such as Norway spruce, Scotch pine, larch and silver fir were first cultivated in Denmark in the late eighteenth century. The custom of using a tree as a symbol of Christmas was first introduced to the Danish people in the early part of the nineteenth century. Today every home in Denmark, however poor the family, must have its own Christmas tree. Tens of thousands of trees are now imported each year from Norway and Sweden. Outside the larger cities it is still not unusual for a man to cut down a tree from his own forest, as the man has done on this Christmas Plate. Often the whole family participates in the selection of the tree, after which it is cut down and then dragged, carried or pulled home on a sled.

Not only is there a tree in every home, but one is also placed in every hospital, hotel, restaurant and store of Denmark. The story for the 1930 Christmas Plate mentions the gigantic tree found each year in the Town Hall Square of Copenhagen. Most of the other cities and towns also have a Christmas tree set up somewhere near the heart of the municipality.

Whenever Danish ships start on a voyage that will keep the sailors away from home at Christmas time, a small tree is usually taken aboard. Then at Christmas the tree is placed at the top of the mast, and the holiday is celebrated at sea. Even though the Danish yachtsman may get little use out of his boat during the winter months, he likes to decorate it at Christmas. He often thinks it as necessary to have a tree tied to the top of his ship's mast, or atop the ship if there is no mast, as it is to have one within his home.

56

The Royal Castle of Amalienborg, Copenhagen
by
Th. Larsen

1914

The Amalienborg is made up of four huge, almost identical palaces in rococo style, enclosing an octagonal "square". The northeast palace serves as the home of King Frederik IX and Queen Ingrid. Another of the palaces is now being repaired and redecorated to be the personal residence of Crown Princess *Margrethe*.

The land for the building of the Amalienborg was given by Frederik V to four relatives with the stipulation that each employ the noted architect, Eigtved, and follow the rococo style of design. The four palaces were built by the noblemen between 1749 and 1760. Frederik V never lived at the Amalienborg as he and his Court preferred the Christiansborg. In 1794 when the Christiansborg was burned the Amalienborg was purchased to house the king and members of the royal family. Ever since that time the Amalienborg has been the official residence of the king.

In the center of the court stands a statue of Frederik V which is considered by experts to be the finest equestrian statue in Northern Europe. The statue was presented to Frederik V in 1770 by the Asiatic Company. Unfortunately, the statue almost caused the company to go bankrupt because of the unexpected great costs, mostly due to the fact that the sculptor, Frenchman Jacques Saly, was so fond of Copenhagen that he deliberately protracted the work to prolong his stay there.

Another famous equestrian statue, this one of Christian V, is located in the center of *Kongens Nytorv* (King's New Market), Copenhagen's largest square. Students come here every June in quaint, yellow, horse-drawn wagons in celebration of their matriculation. At the statue they join hands and circle it three times, shouting their Danish "hurrahs".

58

The Chained Dog Getting a Double Meal on
Christmas Eve
by
Dahl Jensen

1915

In Denmark, as in many countries of the world, the dog has been a popular pet for many generations. On this Christmas Plate is shown a dog, chained to his doghouse, watching the home of his master on Christmas Eve. He can see the Christmas tree through the window and has probably sensed the excitement of the season, especially from the children. Surely he must realize this is a very special night of the year.

The family has not forgotten their canine friend for in the bowl beside him is a double ration of food. It is an old Scandinavian custom that all pets, as well as the farm animals, get double rations on Christmas Eve.

The dog shown is of a somewhat indefinable breed. The artist deliberately painted a dog that would not be of a particular breed as he wanted to portray a common dog. It will soon be illegal in Denmark to keep a dog chained as the one shown, even though he is well treated by the family owning him.

The popularity of dogs as pets in this small country is indicated by the fact that there are now 108 different breeds of dogs registered. The German Shepherd heads the list with 2187 entries, and the Cocker Spaniel comes next with 1570. Of course there are many thousands of dogs in town and country alike which do not qualify for registration because of mixed breeding.

Everyone owning a dog in Denmark must buy a dog tag each year. Dog owners are also required to carry liability insurance.

Christmas Prayer of the Sparrows
by
J. Bloch Jørgensen

1916

On the eastern coast of Zealand are the chalk cliffs called *Stevns Klint.* While these are striking cliffs they are only about one-third as high as those on the island of Møn. The Højerup Church, shown on this plate, was built near the edge of *Stevns Klint* during the latter part of the thirteenth century. Legend says that the church found its foundation being undermined by the sea, and so moved itself a handbreadth inland every Christmas. This retreat must have been too cautious because the cemetery, and finally in 1928 part of the church, toppled into the sea. In recent years the church has been restored and the cliffs below it reinforced with masonry to prevent future damage.

Church building began on a large scale in Denmark around the year 1100. A great majority of the hundreds of large and small churches erected all over the country at that time are in the Romanesque or round-arch style. Many of the early churches were built by the peasants themselves. They were built of granite collected on the spot and there rough-hewn in squares. About the year 1200 the Gothic or pointed-arch style appeared in Denmark. This style of architecture continued, with some modifications, until the middle of the fifteenth century.

About half a century after the start of the extensive church building, the supply of available granite started becoming scarce. Valdemar the Great and Bishop Absalon then showed great foresight by summoning artisans from Northern Italy to teach the Danes how to fire bricks and erect buildings from them. The brick industry still flourishes in Denmark today.

Arrival of the Christmas Boat
by
Achton Friis

1917

Arrival of the Christmas boat refers to the arrival of a boat carrying Americans of Danish descent home to Denmark for the Christmas celebration. The boat is gaily dressed with flags and there is a festive holiday spirit aboard. The harbor is also decorated for the season and bands are playing as the big passenger liner is guided into its berth by tugboats. Some in the happy, smiling, waving crowd on shore must wipe away a tear of joy as they wait to welcome friends and relatives. The newspapers carry names and biographies of some of the Christmas boat passengers. The jubilation is general as most passers-by will join in welcoming the arriving guests. As a rule, all passenger boats coming from America after mid-December are considered Christmas boats.

It is estimated that 170,000 Danes now live abroad, about 100,000 of whom live in the United States and Canada. The majority of those in America have learned the English language and have become naturalized.

Shortly after World War I a society called "The Danish Overseas League" was formed whose objects were to "strengthen the bonds between Denmark and Danes abroad and between them mutually". Christian X did the League the honor of becoming its patron, and King Frederik IX followed when he ascended to the throne. The League sends its monthly *"Danmarksposten"* to some nine thousand members in 110 countries.

Each year on a Sunday in June the League has its summer convention and Danes from all parts of the world gather in the great banquet hall of Kronborg Castle.

The Fishing Boat Returning Home for Christmas
by
Achton Friis

1918

Through the ages fishing has been important to the economy of Denmark. There is fishing off the entire coast and in recent years a sea-going fishing fleet has developed which operates in the North Sea, the Kattegat and the Baltic. The foremost fishing town is Esbjerg on the west coast of Jutland. Here may be found some four miles of quays and several hundred fishing boats. Other important fishing ports include Skagen and Frederikshavn in the extreme northeast of Jutland.

The number of active commercial fishermen is well over 12,000 with another 500 part-time fishermen. The fishing boats range from rowboats and sailboats to large motor vessels equipped with powerful engines. A typical fishing vessel might be a gaff-rigged North Sea cutter as shown on this plate, which is usually operated by four men who work on a profit-sharing basis. The most common varieties caught by the Danish fishermen are cod, haddock, plaice, herring, trout and eel.

The Danish people have long felt a responsibility for conducting marine research and have contributed much to our present knowledge of fish and the sea. One interesting bit of information that required several decades of research pertains to the freshwater eel, varieties of which are found in Denmark and North America. It was finally proven that the freshwater eel breeds in the Sargasso Sea between the West Indies and the Bermudas. Then the young of these two entirely different species, assisted by the ocean currents, migrate to the shores of North America and Europe, where they find their way up the freshwater streams. After growing for several years they start the long trip back to the Sargasso Sea where they spawn and die.

66

Outside the Lighted Window
by
Achton Friis

1919

Once again (as in 1907) Bing & Grøndahl has selected a motif to illustrate the story of *The Little Match Girl* by Hans Christian Andersen.

Although the average Danish family does not yet own an automobile and the many electrical appliances taken for granted by most families in the United States, there is little, if any, poverty in Denmark. This country was the first in the world to introduce efficient social services. Denmark has had an Old Age Pension System since 1891. The basis of modern Danish social legislation is a group of laws passed in 1933 and usually referred to as the Social Reform. The system of social security includes workmen's compensation, accident aid, child welfare, and national insurance through State-approved sick-benefit societies managed by the people themselves.

Today all men over sixty-five years of age and women over sixty are entitled to an old age pension. Most municipalities have built special apartments for pensioners where they can live for a nominal rent.

The health societies provide free medical attention, often free hospital services, and medicines at greatly reduced prices.

Legislation has been passed that guarantees every wage earner an annual vacation of three weeks with pay. Every employer must buy Vacation Stamps at the post office and paste them in a special book every month, at the rate of about six percent of the wages of the employee. If the employee changes his place of employment he takes his book along to his new job. At the time of his annual vacation (sometime between May 2 and Sept. 30) he takes the book to the post office and gets his vacation money.

Hare in the Snow
by
Achton Friis

1920

The hare is one of the more common wild animals of Denmark and is found in almost every part of the country. Other small animals that are fairly plentiful include the marten, squirrel, badger, mole, hedgehog, shrew, weasel and field mouse.

The wolf was once a native of this area, but now is extinct. The only large wild animals remaining today are the deer and fox. Deer and pheasant were introduced into the Danish woods many years ago for sporting purposes. Today the pheasant in particular is prolific. Pheasants and partridges are often seen rising quickly into the air when startled by a fox or other predatory animal. There are many other types of bird life in Denmark, most of which have been mentioned in the story for the 1899 Christmas Plate.

Frogs are plentiful in most of the country, and the stork is often seen wandering around in marsh and meadow catching them to take back to the nest for its greedy young. Among the reptiles are lizards and snakes, including the adder. Insects are numerous in the summer, but disappear in winter, during which time they exist as eggs, larva or cocoon. There, as everywhere in the wake of humans, can be found the common mouse and rat.

Carp is the most common of the freshwater fish, but there are many other species such as pike and perch. Trout and salmon abound in the streams, particularly those of Jutland.

The most common domestic animals are the cow, hog, horse, dog and cat.

Pigeons in the Castle Court
by
Achton Friis

1921

Near the heart of Copenhagen is an island called *Slotsholmen* (Castle Island) formed by canals on all sides. This picturesque island is where fishmongers, members of parliament, stockbrokers, flower merchants and Supreme Court judges conduct their business. Here is Christiansborg Castle which now houses the Danish *Folketing* (Parliament) and the Ministry for Foreign Affairs. The castle is the sixth structure to be built on the site. The first was the castle-fortress built by Bishop Absalon in 1167, the ruins of which can still be seen under the present building. From 1441 until the disastrous fire of 1794 the Christiansborg was used as a royal residence.

Pictured on this plate is the Royal Chapel, connected with the Christiansborg Castle by the Cavalier's Passage. This is still the church of the Danish Navy and the Royal Family. Entombed in the church are two of Denmark's greatest naval heroes. One is the almost legendary Tordenskjold who defeated Charles XII of Sweden during the Great Northern War. The other is Niels Juel who was victorious over the Swedish fleet at Køge in 1677. The chapel is one of the masterpieces of the famous Danish architect C. F. Hansen who also designed the Supreme Court of Justice *(Højesteret),* situated between the Castle and the Royal Chapel in St. George's Court.

Also found on *Slotsholmen* are the Thorvaldsen Museum, the Stock Exchange, the Museum of Armor and the Royal Library. The open-air market where fish, flowers and fresh vegetables may be purchased adds color as well as aroma to the scene.

Star of Bethlehem
by
Achton Friis

1922

When scientists try to explain the star of Bethlehem it becomes difficult because no one knows for sure when Christ was born. It has now been proven that Herod who was king at the time of the birth of Christ actually died about four years before the year we consider to be that of Christ's birth. Archaeologists working in Ankara, Turkey several years ago uncovered an inscription listing the years in which orders were issued for tax collections. Three of the dates were 28 B.C., 8 B.C., and A.D. 14. Historians have ruled out 28 B.C. as being too early, and A.D. 14 as being too late for the taxes for which Mary and Joseph went to Bethlehem to be enrolled. This seems to indicate that Jesus was born in 8 B.C., but in those days travel was slow and communications poor. It would take a year, or more likely two, to get the word to countries, such as Palestine, which were near the edge of the Roman Empire.

The story of the 1901 Christmas Plate tells about the wise men and the star. "The wise men from the east" were probably from a part of the world we formerly called Persia, and were priests of Zoroaster and believers in astrology. They believed that the location of heavenly bodies, particularly the seven ancient planets, influenced the lives of human beings. It is now known, though it probably was not in that day, that once each 805 years Mars, Jupiter and Saturn appear in an extremely close group. Since this last happened in 1604, it would also have occurred in A.D. 799 and 6 B.C. This could easily have been accepted by the wise men as the sign for which they had long searched the sky.

Many Christians prefer to think of the star of Bethlehem as a miracle that cannot be explained. Certainly the important thing is not the star, but the Christmas story itself.

The Royal Hunting Castle, the Ermitage
by
Achton Friis

1923

Although Christian V enclosed the Klampenborg Deer Park for hunting purposes, it was Christian VI who built the small palace in the park called the *Eremitage* (Hermitage, or sometimes called the Royal Hunting Castle). Designed by Laurids de Thura and built in 1736, the castle is Christian VI's finest existing edifice. It is situated in the center of the Deer Park in a particularly beautiful area known as *Eremitagen Sletten* (Hermitage Plain). Being about one hundred thirty feet above sea level, the castle commands magnificient views of a large part of Northern Zealand and of the passing ships in the Sound. The influence of Viennese baroque is shown by the fine marble chimney pieces, gilt carvings and ceilings. Numerous nude statues decorate the gracefully curving roof.

Herds of one hundred or more deer can often be seen in the vicinity of the *Eremitage*. In all there are more than twelve hundred fallow and red deer in the park, many of which are relatively tame.

The Hermitage derived its name from the fact that King Christian VI sometimes wanted to be alone. At such times he would have his meals sent down by dumbwaiter from the kitchen direct to his private dining room.

Several years ago when Queen Elizabeth and Prince Philip of Great Britain paid a visit to King Frederik IX and Queen Ingrid, they lunched at Hermitage Castle.

The castle is still used by the royal hunting party at the annual hunt arranged by the King. The park is closed to the public on that day, but on the other 364 days of the year it belongs to the Danish people.

Lighthouse in Danish Waters
by
Achton Friis

1924

Denmark has a large number of lighthouses for a country of its size. Excluding Greenland and the Faroe Islands, the land area of Denmark is 16,576 square miles, or about half that of the state of Maine. This land area is made up of the peninsula of Jutland which adjoins Germany, and approximately five hundred islands, about one hundred of which are populated. A study of the map on page 17 makes it easy to understand why it has been necessary to erect many lighthouses and other aids to navigation.

The two largest islands are Zealand and Funen. Copenhagen, Denmark's capital and largest city, is in Zealand. In Funen is the city of Odense, famed for being the birthplace of Hans Christian Andersen. The Great Belt flows between the two islands. Pictured on this plate is the Sprøgo Lighthouse on the island of Sprøgo located in the Great Belt about midway between Korsør and Nyborg.

In the early part of the last century, navigation was made comparatively safe through the Sound (the water between Denmark and Sweden), but very little was done in the Great Belt because it was easier to levy custom duties and light dues on foreign ships at Elsinore. (See story for 1950 plate.) As shipping rapidly increased, however, lighthouses and other navigational aids were added in the western part of the country. C. F. Grove, head of the Danish Lighthouse Service from 1852-1883 did much to modernize the lighthouses. He replaced the old-fashioned coal-burning lights with revolving reflectors. He also erected twenty-four new lighthouses at strategic points and placed eight lightships in Danish waters.

The Child's Christmas
by
Achton Friis

1925

Every married couple derives a special joy out of the first Christmas of their first-born child. It is true that the child is too young to understand why Christmas is celebrated . . . too young to enjoy his gifts as he will during later Christmases, but he is not too young to give a new meaning to Christmas for the parents. It is easy to imagine the thoughts of this young couple as they look at the child and his first Christmas tree. They are dreaming of later Christmases . . . later children . . . and, too, they are rejoicing for the wonderful things this Christmas time has brought to them. It is a moment they will long remember.

The Danes have their big family dinner and gift exchange on Christmas Eve. Christmas Day is observed rather quietly but the next day, generally referred to as the Second Christmas Day, is given over to gaiety and entertainment. Many people spend the day going from house to house to visit friends and to *skaale* or drink healths to them. The evening is often spent at the theater.

Christmas is the oldest of Nordic festivals, and it is steeped in old tradition. Long before the birth of Christ a pagan festival of several days duration was held around the shortest day of the year. Bonfires and offerings were made to appease "evil powers", but even in that heathen era gentleness, gifts and peace belonged to the celebration. To this day some Christmas customs are not altogether free from the influence of both old heathen and early Christian traditions. Some old folks still remember when it was considered quite dangerous to venture out on Christmas Night because it was believed that evil spirits roamed freely on that night.

80

Churchgoers on Christmas Day
by
Achton Friis

1926

The artist of this plate was inspired by the Haraldsted Church situated in the town of the same name, a few miles north of Ringsted in Zealand. This church contains the body of the Danish nobleman Knud Lavard who was murdered in the woods of Haraldsted on January 6, 1131, while on a visit to his relative Cecilia (daughter of King Canute the Holy) and her husband Earl Eric. Legend persists that a holy spring with curative powers gushed forth on the spot where the crime was committed. In 1146 a chapel was built near the spring, and in 1956-1957 a modern concrete Lutheran Church was erected here and named for Knud Lavard.

Some ninety-seven to ninety-eight percent of the population of Denmark now belongs to the Lutheran Church, though far from this number could be called regular churchgoers. Other churches include the Methodist, Mosaic Community, Reformed, Baptist, Church of England, Orthodox Russian and Roman Catholic. These churches are generally divided into two groups – the recognized and the non-recognized. The ministers of the recognized group have been authorized to perform ecclesiastical rites which have civil validity. The non-recognized group may use the chapels of the National Church for funerals, but their clergy cannot perform legally valid marriages and baptisms.

The National Church is financed from funds vested in it in former times by Treasury grants as laid down in legislation, and by taxes levied on members along lines similar to those which apply to income tax. Resignation from the National Church secures exemption from the latter tax.

Skating Couple
by
Achton Friis

1927

No one in Denmark lives more than forty miles from the sea which possibly explains why the Danish people have long participated in aquatic sports. Ice skating, shown on this Christmas Plate, has been enjoyed in Denmark for many centuries.

The national game of Denmark is football (soccer). There are many football clubs scattered over the country which not only compete with each other but have competed internationally. Other sports in which the Danes have done well in international competitions include rowing, swimming, sailing, badminton, tennis, handball, archery, fencing and road cycling. Since the average family in Denmark does not own an automobile, cycling, as well as being a sport, is the common mode of transportation for men, women and children. Inasmuch as Denmark is relatively level, cycling demands no heavy exertion and it permits the people to travel at what they feel is a reasonable speed. Everyone in Denmark rides a bicycle – even the cabinet members, the bishops, and the King and Queen.

Although the desire to win at any sport is great, the Danes do not allow it to deprive them of enjoyment from the sport for its own sake. Boxing and cycling are the only two sports that are commercialized at all. The Danish people participate in sports for the fun derived. Their love of fun and good humor is illustrated by the well-known story of the Dane who went to Norway to ski. He was attempting to put on skis for the first time. A Norwegian passing by tried to be helpful by saying, "You have those skis turned the wrong way". The Dane retorted, "Just how do you know which way I'm going?"

84

*Eskimos Looking at the Church of Their
Little Village in Greenland
by
Achton Friis*

1928

The connection between Scandinavia and Greenland goes back to the hardy Vikings who made voyages to North America by way of Greenland five hundred years before Columbus. The modern colonization of Greenland dates back to 1721 with the arrival of the Danish missionary, Hans Egede. Egede must have been persuasive because today the total population of about 25,000 belong to the National Lutheran Church of Denmark. The Greenlanders are largely descended from Eskimos who probably migrated from North America. The common language is still Eskimo, although Danish is also now being taught in the schools. It is interesting to note that the radio broadcasting system of Greenland, which since 1958 penetrates the entire inhabited area, can be heard and understood by the North American Eskimos.

Excluding the continent of Australia, Greenland is the largest island in the world, being about fifty times as large as the rest of Denmark put together. Five-sixths of the area, however, is covered by the vast ice-cap which has a thickness of up to 10,000 feet. Only a narrow coastal fringe is ice free, and even there forests are non-existent. The economy is based largely upon the sea. For many years seal was abundant and supplied most of the needs of the people. In recent years, though, the surrounding waters have become warmer and the seal have moved elsewhere. In their place have come codfish, in numbers unparalleled anywhere else.

The only farming done is some sheep raising in the extreme southwest area. There is also some mining of cryolite, zinc and lead in Greenland.

Fox Outside Farm on Christmas Eve
by
Achton Friis

1929

The farm shown on this Christmas Plate is probably located in Northern Zealand or Eastern Jutland for it is in these two sections that a fox is more likely to be seen. Actually there are not many large wild animals left in Denmark today. The largest to be found, outside of zoological gardens, are the red deer, the roe deer and the fox. Hundreds of years ago there were several other species of large animals in this area but either they have died out because of the difficult conditions for existence, or were all killed before the current strict laws to conserve the wildlife of Denmark.

Three-fourths of Denmark's land is used for agricultural purposes. The average farm in Denmark today has about thirty-seven acres and is worked by the owner. Tenant farming here is the exception. In many cases, however, the small farmer owns only the farm buildings and pays an annual rent for the land which remains the property of the State. Farming here is more general than specialized as most farmers raise a variety of livestock and crops.

Danish farming is well organized through co-operative associations owned and controlled by the farmers themselves. These co-operatives have done much to help the farmers in marketing their products, maintaining quality for which the Danes have become famous, and in many cases, turning the raw product into a marketable one.

The government promotes Danish agriculture by running experimental farms, and by establishing certain levels for quality of products to be exported.

The Yule Tree in the Town Hall Square of Copenhagen
by
H. Flügenring

1930

The *Raadhusplads* (Town Hall Square) might well be called the hub of Copenhagen. Here is the heart of the business and entertainment district. The second square of importance is *Kongens Nytorv* (The King's New Market), center of the so-called aristocratic quarter with the embassies and legations, the Royal Theater, and the more expensive, though older, apartment houses. These two important squares are connected by a mile-long series of five streets known collectively as the *Strøget* (the Stretch).

Every Christmas in front of the *Raadhus* (Town Hall) is placed a tall, beautiful tree. It is here in this square that friends like to meet in the weeks before Christmas to admire the tree with its myriad of lights and to wish each other a joyous holiday season.

There are other times when the Square is the gathering place of large groups. On the night of a general election, crowds gather there to read the election results posted on the front of the big newspaper offices. It was here that the people gathered that wonderful, memorable evening of May 4, 1945, when the news came that Denmark was being liberated.

Copenhagen has often been called "The City of Spires". The Town Hall, the building on the right of the Christmas tree as shown on this plate, has the distinction of having the highest tower in the city. It is 346 feet high and houses the Town Hall clock from which is heard every quarter hour the tune of the old night watchmen's call. The entire building is elaborately decorated both inside and outside with sculptures and paintings.

Arrival of the Christmas Train
by
Achton Friis

1931

The Arrival of the Christmas Train was painted by the same artist who portrayed the arrival of the Christmas boat on the 1917 plate. The custom of meeting the Christmas trains and Christmas boats with special ceremonies has been in effect in Denmark for a long time. Shown on this plate is a group of happy Danes as they await the train, pulling into the station with relatives and friends from distant parts of the country. The railway stations are always decorated for Christmas and even the trains hint of the season.

Denmark's first railroad dates back to 1847 when the line from Copenhagen to Roskilde was inaugurated. Railroads were introduced in Jutland in 1862. Today the country has a dense network of approximately 3170 miles of railroad tracks, 1650 of which are operated by the Danish State Railways and the rest by private companies in which the State or municipalities have a financial interest. There are a sufficient number of trains to seat about 135,000 passengers, and the network boasts well over four hundred railway stations. The trains are operated by electric, steam or diesel-electric power. Whether measured by the area of the country or by the number of inhabitants, the Danish railway network is highly developed.

Most of the bridges connecting the various islands carry both railway and highway traffic. The trains must be put aboard ferries to cross the Great Belt.

In recent years it has been necessary for the railroads to make many improvements in their services because of the ever-increasing competition on the part of motor vehicles.

92

Lifeboat at Work
by
H. Flügenring

1932

Since Denmark is largely an insular country, the sea has ever played an important part in its history. The Vikings once controlled the seas as well as a large part of the civilized world. A tranquil sea is shown on several Christmas Plates, but this is the first plate to indicate the power of a raging sea.

This painting shows a typical lifeboat of Skagen, the northernmost town in Denmark, located at the extreme top of Jutland. Many lives have been saved through the gallant efforts of the crews of these lifeboats. They are usually called upon to perform their services when the sea is raging at its worst. Unfortunately, these crews have not always succeeded in getting themselves safely back. The sea in this area is always rough because the waters of the North Sea and those of the Kattegat fight a never-ceasing battle, and the lifeboat crews must often go out in an attempt to save lives. Skagen and Fred-erikshavn (a few miles south of Skagen) are two of the more important commercial fishing centers of the coun-try. Many fishing boats operate out of these two towns, fishing the Skagerrak, the Kattegat, the North Sea and even the Barents Sea.

When the artist painted the scene shown on this plate he was remembering the accident that happened Au-gust 5, 1930, not far from Skagen. The American boat *"Chickasaw"* collided with the Swedish steamer *"Femern"* with the result that the forward part of the *"Femern"* was cut off and sank with four crewmen aboard. The rest of the ship was towed into the harbor of Frederikshavn.

The Korsør-Nyborg Ferry
by
H. Flügenring

1933

Those in charge of the first Danish railways soon realized that the efficiency of this new means of transportation would necessitate the use of ferries to cross the Sounds and Belts that separate the various parts of the Danish railway network. The Danish State Railways opened the first ferry service between Fredericia and Strib in 1872. These ferries, carrying only a single-track, were discontinued when the Little Belt Bridge (shown on 1935 plate) was completed.

The ferry service across the Great Belt began in 1883 with ferries running between Korsør and Nyborg. Paddle wheel driven ferryboats with a double-track were used at first, but today a series of modern ferries, among the greatest in the world, are employed.

The motor vessel *Zealand*, pictured on this plate, was built in 1933 and used to transport trains, automobiles, cargo and passengers across the Great Belt. During the occupation in World War II, the Germans blew up the ship in retaliation of the sabotage done to German transports, et cetera, by the Danish Underground Movement (see story for 1940 plate). After the war the boat was repaired and is still in service today.

The ferry service between Zealand and Funen is now in two parts. The Nyborg-Korsør route is used largely for the transport of trains and conveyance of goods, while autombiles are transported between nearby Knudshoved and Halsskov. The ferry trip takes about one hour.

The Great Belt is seventy miles long and about twenty miles wide with a channel extending from north to south.

Church Bell in Tower
by
Immanuel Tjerne

1934

Christmas Eve is the big event of the year in Denmark. Beginning at noon the shops, restaurants and other business establishments progressively close so that their employees may go home and prepare for the Christmas Eve activities.

At five o'clock the church bells in town and country ring out to summon the people to worship. The artist of this plate pictures the old-fashioned way in which the bells are rung in most village churches. The bell-ringer is, as a rule, someone hired to do the job, often a devoted church member who derives great pleasure from ringing the bell, particularly at Christmas. Everyone makes a special effort to attend the impressive church service on Christmas Eve, even those who seldom or never go at other times.

The Danes hope for a white Christmas, and often have it. If it has not already snowed, it seems frequently to start when the church bells begin to ring.

The Christmas Eve service begins shortly after five o'clock. The church is always beautifully decorated with evergreens and lighted by many candles. The minister is dressed in a black robe with a big white Elizabethan ruff. The service is opened by a layman, the choirdeacon, in full evening dress. The crowded congregation includes many children anxious for the Christmas Eve festivities that will take place later in the evening. In front of the chancel stand several Christmas trees, their branches loaded with lighted candles. A solemn Boy Scout in uniform walks around each tree all during the service to make sure it does not catch fire.

98

The Lillebelt *Bridge Connecting Funen with Jutland*
by
Ove Larsen

1935

It is easy to understand why the motif for this Christmas Plate was chosen. The Danes are proud of their many bridges that span the waterways between many of their islands. Although the *Lillebelt* (Little Belt) Bridge was started in 1929, it was not opened to traffic until 1935.

The bridge connects Middelfart in Funen with Fredericia in Jutland. The main point of interest in Middelfart is the Folk Museum. Fredericia was established over three hundred years ago as a staunch fortress and the ramparts of the old walled town still stand. The town was fortified to protect the Jutland peninsula which contains about three-fourths of Denmark's land. Today Fredericia is Denmark's most important railway junction and still remains a garrison town.

At its widest point the Little Belt is eighteen miles across, but is narrowest near the bridge. The water at this point, though, is unusually deep and the current quite strong. The cost of building the bridge was about thirty-two million Danish kroner which is over four million U.S. dollars at today's rate of exchange. The bridge is almost three-fourths of a mile long and stands 108 feet above water. The construction of the bridge required some fifteen thousand tons of steel and well over a million cubic feet of Danish cement. In addition to a roadway and pedestrian lane the bridge supports a double railroad track. This Christmas Plate shows a train crossing the bridge shortly after it was opened.

Although the Danes are justifiably proud of the Little Belt Bridge, the pride of the Danish engineers is really the Storström Bridge. Two miles long, this bridge connects the island of Falster to Zealand, and is one of the longest bridges in all Europe.

100

Royal Guard Outside Amalienborg Castle
in Copenhagen
by
Ove Larsen

1936

Whenever the King is in town a small crowd gathers at noon around the green bronze equestrian statue of Christian V (see 1914 plate) to await the ceremony of the Change of the Royal Guard. The Guard takes a long route from the Royal Barracks to Amalienborg. This is done to give more people a chance to watch the Guard as it marches along. The Danish people never tire of the sight, and take great delight in showing off the Royal Guard to their foreign visitors.

It is truly a picturesque sight! There are thirty-six young men, drafted from among the tallest in the country, dressed in light blue trousers and dark blue coats, glistening with polished buttons and crossed with breast straps. Wearing enormous black busbies, they march briskly along to the music of a thirty-one piece band. On special days such as holidays and the King's birthday, the Guard parades in full dress scarlet uniform.

When the Guard reaches Amalienborg Court, there is much saluting and flashing of officers' swords. The band then forms itself into a ring and gives a short midday concert under the king's windows. After the music the *Dannebrog* is then ceremoniously brought from the palace as the men in the crowd bare their heads. The band then leads the retiring Guard back to the barracks by a more direct route.

On the left of this plate and in the background may be seen Frederik's Church, also known as the Marble Church. The internal diameter of the dome is ninety-eight feet, only a few feet less than that of St. Peter's in Rome. For lack of money, Frederik's Church remained in an unfinished condition from 1770 to 1894 when it was completed at the expense of C. F. Tietgen, a wealthy banker.

Arrival of Christmas Guests
by
Ove Larsen

1937

This intra-city bus is bringing family and friends to the Christmas Night party. It is easy to detect the joy with which the guests are being greeted. The starlit night and deep snow provide an impressive and peaceful setting that makes for a joyous Christmas season.

The country has good inter-city bus service, owned and operated largely by the Danish State Railways who introduced their bus service in 1932. The first buses were initiated to replace some discontinued railway lines in the southern part of Jutland, and later the service was extended to the more outlying areas. The Danish State Railways have endeavored to acquire bus lines running parallel to their railway lines. They have been able to operate the railways far more economically by occasionally replacing little-used railway lines with bus service. The bus routes today number more than eleven hundred and cover a total of twenty thousand miles as they crisscross the country. Many buses carry mail and small parcels as well as passengers. Almost all of them provide means for carrying bicycles on the back or on top. Many of the buses on longer trips have hostesses who assist the passengers and point out places of interest.

The church in the background is just one of many dating back to the Middle Ages when Catholicism was still the predominant religion. After the Reformation these churches were taken over by the State to be used as Lutheran Churches. Many relics from the Catholic period are preserved and meticulously cared for because they represent a part of Danish church history.

Lighting the Candles
by
Immanuel Tjerne

This is one of the most original of all the Christmas Plates. It shows the entire country of Denmark lighted by candles, thus wishing everyone a *Glaedelig Jul* (Happy Christmas).

In painting the six candles on top of Jutland and Zealand, the artist had in mind an old celebration that took place very early in the morning on December 13 which before the Gregorian calendar was considered to be the shortest day of the year. The day was sometimes called "little Yule" because many considered it to be the beginning of the Christmas season. In Sweden, a young girl – the prettiest one of the household – was dressed in a white robe with a red sash to impersonate the Lucia bride. On her head she wore a wire crown covered with whortleberry twigs and fastened in it were several candles. At the first cockcrow, between one and four o'clock, the candles were lighted and the Lucia bride went through the house, awakening all those who were sleeping. She served them either a sweet drink or a cup of coffee, and sang a special song. Everyone called her *Lussi* (Lucia bride).

The custom, with some changes, has now been adopted in Denmark. Young girls are dressed in white as Lucia brides and wearing their crown of lighted candles, visit the hospitals on Christmas Day. There they sing Christmas carols and hymns to the patients.

The name *Lucia* is derived from Saint Lucia who according to legend died as a martyr in Syracuse about A.D. 300. The name was connected with *lux* (light) and St. Lucia's Day was celebrated as a festival of lights.

Ole Lock-Eye, the Sandman
by
Immanuel Tjerne

1939

Hans Christian Andersen's charming fairy tale entitled *"Ole Lukoie"* (Ole Lock-Eye) was first published in 1842. Ole Lock-Eye is an imaginary character, a dream elf, who comes around each night to make children sleepy. He comes in very quietly for he walks in his socks. He sprinkles a tiny bit of sand in the children's eyes to keep them closed so he will not be seen. Then he tiptoes behind them and breathes softly on their necks to make them sleepier. He wants them to go to sleep so he can tell them stories because Ole Lock-Eye knows more stories than anyone else on earth and he likes to tell them.

Ole Lock-Eye is always handsomely dressed in a coat of silk, but it would be impossible to say what color it is because it seems to change color as he moves about the room. Under one arm he carries a plain umbrella and under the other, umbrellas with pictures on them. If the child has been good all day, Ole Lock-Eye holds an umbrella with pictures over the bed and the child is transported into a land of fantastic dreams. When the child has been naughty, Ole Lock-Eye holds the plain umbrella over him. Then the child sleeps restlessly and does not dream at all.

In Andersen's story, Ole Lock-Eye comes every evening for a week to visit a little boy named Hjalmer. Each night, Monday through Sunday, he takes Hjalmer on exciting adventures that would thrill any child.

This Christmas Plate depicts Ole Lock-Eye as he holds the umbrella with pictures over a well behaved child. The Christmas tree in the corner gives a hint of some of the wonderful dreams the child may be having.

Delivering Christmas Letters
by
Ove Larsen

1940

Although Denmark was at peace when this Christmas Plate was designed, World War II was already in progress. Perhaps the artist was thinking of the many mothers who were then meeting the postman each day in the hope that he would bring a letter from a dear one. The postmen in Denmark wear bright red coats that lend a splash of color to city streets on the grayest of days. The letter-boxes are all painted red and on each is the coach horn, which was used on the old stage-coaches and now is a symbol of Scandinavian postal services.

Denmark, having retained her neutrality in World War I, hoped to do the same during World War II. Although she had signed a non-aggression treaty with Hitler, German troops marched into Copenhagen in April, 1940, and within hours the country was in a state of occupation.

The year 1943 marked the end of the cooperation between Denmark and Nazi-Germany. The underground Resistance Movement in Denmark had been building up since 1941 and was now strong enough to exert influence. By the end of the war the Resistance had organized a military force of 56,000 men, and its sabotage groups had accomplished thousands of major operations against rail lines, factories working for the Germans, German military installations and depots, ports, shipyards and ships. It published and circulated some 235 million copies of illegal newspapers during the occupation. Truly the Resistance did much to help the cause of the Allies.

Horses Enjoying Christmas Meal in Stable
by
Ove Larsen

1941

These horses are enjoying the double ration that the Scandinavians customarily give to all farm animals and household pets at Christmas time. The birds, watching as the horses eat, hope for a chance to grab a few seeds for themselves.

These horses are of the Oldenburg breed, a type of workhorse. Denmark's other common breeds of workhorses include the heavy Jutland, the light Frederiksborg and the heavy Belgian horse. The Norwegian pony is rather common on the very small farms.

The number of horses in Denmark is rapidly decreasing. This is because the agricultural industry is becoming more and more mechanized. Within the foreseeable future, work horses will probably be completely replaced by tractors, and farmers will keep such horses only out of respect or for their personal pleasure.

Horse shows are held all over the country. There is an annual country fair at the *Bellahøj* in the northern part of Copenhagen. Here farmers show their best cattle, horses, et cetera, and prizes are awarded to those exhibiting the best animals.

There are also many fine race horses in Denmark. Horse racing here dates back to the latter part of the eighteenth century. The Danish Derby, the earliest of the Scandinavian Derby Races, was inaugurated in 1875. Today there are several race tracks in the country, the most important of which is *Galopbanen* in the Klampenborg Woods (see stories for 1905 and 1923 plates). Betting is government controlled and bookmaking is illegal.

Danish Farm on Christmas Night
by
Ove Larsen

1942

Denmark has always been an agricultural country. The climate is favorable and the soil is easy to till, though not particularly fertile. The Danes have long known the value of using fertilizer, and import many tons each year. It is normally purchased by one of the many co-operative associations owned by the farmers, thereby eliminating the profits of the middle man.

During the German occupation the Danish farmers could not get fertilizer and the soil became very poor, causing production per acre to drop considerably. It was also impossible to import fodder and grain needed to feed the cows, hogs and chickens. In many cases it was necessary for the farmer to reduce the number in his herd because of the lack of feed. After the war it required several years for the farmers to get the soil back in condition, their herds of livestock built up again, and farm machinery repaired or replaced.

Today about one-fourth of the population makes its living by farming. The Danish farmer never becomes satisfied with his production records, whether they pertain to bushels of wheat per acre or pounds of butter per cow. He is constantly looking for ways of increasing both quantity and quality of his products. He can keep abreast of the latest agricultural developments by attending one of the twenty-seven agricultural schools scattered over the country that have classes for several months beginning November 1 each year. The 4-H movement, introduced from the United States, has become popular in recent years.

114

The Ribe Cathedral
by
Ove Larsen

115

1943

The oldest cathedral in Denmark and possibly in all Scandinavia is located in Ribe. About the year 850 Ansgar who brought Christianity to the North built a wooden church where today the Ribe Cathedral stands. In 1160 the cathedral was rebuilt of volcanic stone carried to this rockless village by ship from the banks of the Rhine. A brick tower, designed for a stronghold and lookout, was added about 1250. The interior of the church presents an interesting union of Romanesque and Gothic architecture.

The history of Ribe, Denmark's oldest town, goes back at least a thousand years. It was once the chief seaport town on the western coast of Denmark, but the sea receded and silt filled the harbors until Ribe is four miles from the sea. The Danish people make an effort to preserve the ancient character of this little town. As they have for hundreds of years, the cathedral bells still ring four times a day to call the people to prayer. The streets are winding and cobbled, the roofs often sag, the windows are set askew, and the charm of the irregular delights. Here is seen the milk wagon with spigots on the back where housewives gather with pitchers to obtain milk and exchange the latest gossip. Here too can still be heard the voice of the town crier.

Ribe is renown for its storks. According to legend good fortune will come to the household with storks nesting on its roof. For this reason the townspeople vie with one another in trying to attract the birds by placing on their roofs various types of wooden foundations and baskets for nests. The storks winter in Africa and, unfortunately, the number returning to Denmark for the summer is diminishing each year.

116

The Sorgenfri *Castle*
by
Ove Larsen

1944

This Christmas Plate has aptly been called a protest in porcelain against the Nazi invaders. When the Germans occupied Denmark in 1940 they took King Christian X prisoner. Later he was confined to the *Sorgenfri* Castle in Lyngby, just outside Copenhagen. In 1943 a German soldier fired a shot at the King as he sat near a window. The bullet missed its goal, but the windowpane through which it passed is now kept as a souvenir in the Rosenborg Castle collection. The great love and respect the Danish people had for Christian X was manifested by this plate.

The *Sorgenfri* (Carefree) Castle was built in 1705 by Fr. Dieussart for Count Ahlefeldt. In 1734 it was enlarged by the famous architect, Thura, as a summer residence for Frederik V, then crown prince. It was here that King Frederik IX was born in 1899. The castle is now the home of Prince Knud, brother of King Frederik IX, and Princess Caroline-Mathilde.

Nearby the *Sorgenfri* Castle is the extremely interesting *Frilandsmusaet* (Open-Air Museum), started in 1900 by Bernhard Olsen, then director of Tivoli, Copenhagen's famous amusement park. Olsen wished to create, for the enjoyment and education of the Danish people and their posterity, a park where examples of typical Danish architecture could be preserved. The Open-Air Museum continues to grow as farmhouses and buildings of various types are acquired in all parts of Denmark and transported to Lyngby. There they are re-erected to display characteristics of the part of Denmark from which they come. Every building is completely and authentically furnished.

The Old Water Mill
by
Ove Larsen

1945

The picturesque manner in which the old romantic water mills always seem to blend with the landscape has long inspired artists and poets. The water mill shown here is typical of those found in Denmark. Many such mills are still in use and provide an economical means of grinding grain. The water mill superseded the old method of crushing grain by pounding it in a stone or wooden bowl.

Water mills were always built beside, or over, a stream where an appreciable amount of waterfall could be obtained by damming up the stream. One method of obtaining power from the water is to have a large vertically-mounted wheel with buckets on its periphery which fill with water on one side of the wheel, thus causing it to rotate. Another method is to use a wheel mounted horizontally or vertically with paddles extending into a swift moving flow of water. In either case a shaft, often of wood and extending from the wheel into the mill, drives a large stone wheel against a similar stationary one in which grain is fed through a hole in the center. The rubbing action of the two stone wheels against the grain grinds it to a fine meal or flour.

Today there are very few water mills in use in the United States as they have almost entirely been replaced by hammer mills and the large modern flour mills that can blend several types of grain in the correct proportions to produce the many types of bread, cake and pastry mixes now available. There are some people, through, who believe that grain ground by these old water mills makes tastier and more nutritious bread than that made of flour from today's highly developed mills.

Commemoration Cross in Honor of Danish Sailors
Who Lost Their Lives During World War II
by
Margrethe Hyldahl

1946

Immediately after Denmark was invaded, the German leaders commanded shipowners to order their vessels to the nearest neutral port. Most of the captains, realizing the shipowners were forced to give these orders, proceeded at once to set course for the nearest Allied port. There was about 750,000 tons of Danish shipping scattered over the globe at the time. Within a few months almost 200 Danish ships and 5000 Danish seamen were sailing for the Allied cause and as Anthony Eden put it "sharing all the perils of war at sea".

Most of the ships headed for British shores. This greatly benefited Great Britain because shortage of tonnage was one of her serious weaknesses. In the beginning these ships sailed under the British flag. The Danish seamen, however, were anxious to sail under their own flag, and beginning on New Year's Day, 1943, they were allowed to fly the *Dannebrog*. Permission was also granted for the Danish flag to be flown on four British mine sweepers, manned entirely by Danish seamen. On that early June morning in 1944 when the Allied Forces were crossing the Channel toward the coast of Normandy a number of ships were flying the Danish flag.

Of the 5000 Danish sailors who fought for the Allied cause, 1400 lost their lives. In one of the main squares of Copenhagen, overlooking a canal of the harbor, a simple but beautiful oak cross was set up in memory of those men who gave their lives fighting for the freedom of their country and the democratic world. On August 29, 1951, the cross was replaced by an iron anchor.

The Dybbøl Mill
by
Margrethe Hyldahl

Only where Jutland joins Germany does Danish soil touch that of another nation. This area, populated by both Germans and Danes, has for more than a hundred years presented problems and frictions. From ancient times the two provinces of Schleswig and Holstein belonged to Denmark, but Holstein was also considered a member of the German Confederation. In 1848 a war was fought to determine who owned the two provinces, and the Danes were victorious. The Danish victory was short-lived, however, because in 1864, Bismarck, the new leader of Prussia persuaded Austria to join him to again fight for Schleswig and Holstein. As before, the battle was fought in the vicinity of Dybbøl Mill. The Danes fought heroically against overwhelmingly great odds, but in the end five thousand Danes lay dead and Bismarck was victorious. Denmark was forced to cede both provinces, thereby losing a large amount of land and a million inhabitants, about 200,000 of whom were Danes living in Northern Schleswig. Prussia promised that a plebiscite would later determine the fate of North Schleswig, but this promise was never kept. After World War I, the terms of the Treaty of Versailles stated that Schleswig should be divided into three zones, each of which would hold a plebiscite and let the people themselves decide whether they would be German or Danish. The northern one of the three sections voted to return to Denmark. The other two sections preferred to remain German.

The historic Dybbøl Mill near Sonderborg is a symbol of the unconquerable spirit of the Danish people. It has been destroyed and rebuilt several times. Today it is a national museum and the Danes consider the ground around it to be sacred.

"Watchman", Sculpture of Town Hall of Copenhagen
by
Margrethe Hyldahl

125

1948

The present Town Hall of Copenhagen, the sixth of which the city has had, is a comparatively new building. It was designed by Martin Nyrop and built in 1892-1905. The building is mammoth, being 420 feet long and 233 feet wide. The attractive structure is made of red brick, along with some granite, limestone and terra cotta. Above the main entrance is a bronze relief of Bishop Absalon, founder of Copenhagen.

While the 1930 Christmas Plate shows the front of the Town Hall, this plate depicts one of a row of figures along the roof representing the ancient watchmen of the city. The watchman is holding a war weapon of the times, a long-handled mace, and blowing a lur. Although the lur dates back about three thousand years as a musical instrument of Denmark, today it is seldom heard or seen. The lurs, however, are pictured in the trademark used to identify Danish butter and other agricultural products.

Inside the Town Hall may be found the first World Clock, invented and built by Jens Olsen. This clock is one of the most unique in the world, giving all zone times as well as astronomic constellations. The imposing Assembly Hall with an area of 11,250 square feet contains marble busts of Nyrop, Thorvaldsen (see story for 1953 plate) and Andersen (see story for 1954 plate). The Town Hall also houses the local government offices and the Town Museum. This museum traces the history and appearance of Copenhagen through the ages with exhibits of signboards, parts of buildings, guild relics, clothes, paintings and engravings.

Much of Copenhagen and the surrounding countryside can be seen from the 346-foot tower of Town Hall.

Landsoldaten, *Danish Soldier from the
Nineteenth Century
by
Margrethe Hyldahl*

1949

The Danish word *Landsoldaten* was used during the last century in the same way as the modern expression "G.I." is used in the United States. Both terms refer to an enlisted soldier. The statue painted on this plate is in the town of Fredericia in Jutland. It was erected in memory of those who fought in the 1848-1850 war against Germany (see story for 1947 plate).

The statue was made by the well-known sculptor Herman Vilhelm Bissen (1798-1868). The talented young sculptor was awarded the great Gold Medal of the Royal Academy of Art in Copenhagen after he went to Rome and became a most loyal and appreciated assistant to the great Danish sculptor, Bertel Thorvaldsen (see story for 1952 plate). Bissen was responsible for the Mainz statue of Gutenberg. Several of his works can be found in Copenhagen including the statue of King Frederik VI in the Frederiksberg Gardens, the Frederik VII equestrian statue in front of Christiansborg Palace, and the statue of Moses in front of the Church of Our Lady.

The town of Fredericia contains a number of national memorials from past wars with Germany. It is an old town as its charter dates back to 1650 when a decision was made to build a fort there. The inner town still has a network of streets with right angle turns and high ramparts. Fredericia has often in the past given refuge to many who were being persecuted for religious reasons. Many descendants of the French Huguenots may be found in the general area.

There is now a hotel in Fredericia named *Landsoldaten.* The word is sometimes translated as *valiant soldier.*

Kronborg Castle at Elsinore
by
Margrethe Hyldahl

1950

In 1430 Erik of Pomerania, then King of Denmark, decided to impose "Sound Dues" on all vessels entering or leaving the Baltic through the Sound. In order to enforce payment, he built a fortress-castle called *Krogen* at the narrowest part of the Sound, only three miles from Sweden. The method of assessing taxes was both simple and effective. The captain of each vessel was forced to submit a list of all cargo and its value. It was seldom that the captain was tempted to underestimate the value of his ship's goods because it was the king's prerogative to purchase the whole, or any part, of the cargo at the value declared by the captain. For more than four hundred years these dues formed an important part of Denmark's national income.

Between 1574 and 1584 Frederik II built Kronborg Castle where *Krogen* had stood. Originally built of brick, the castle was later encased in sandstone. It was partially destroyed by fire in 1629, and again suffered damage from Swedish bombardment in 1658. In 1857 the dues were abolished when the nations using the Sound agreed to pay Denmark a total of twenty-six million dollars. The silver coins in the coffer of the Kronborg Customs House at that time were later cast into the silver lions which are today seen at the Knight's Hall of Rosenborg Castle.

Shakespeare made the castle near Elsinore forever famous when he chose it as the scene for his drama *Hamlet*. *Hamlet* has been performed here numerous times from 1816 to the present day.

The Museum of Trade and Commerce is now housed in Kronborg Castle.

Jens Bang, *New Passenger Boat Running
Between Copenhagen and Aalborg
by
Margrethe Hyldahl*

1951

The *Jens Bang,* a ferryboat running between Copenhagen and Aalborg in North Jutland, was launched in 1950 and has a displacement of 3284 gross tons.

The ship was named in honor of the great merchant Jens Bang who died in 1644. In 1605 Bang took out a trade license in Aalborg and gradually became one of the most important merchants of his time. He owned many ships and traded with Norway, the Baltic countries, France, Spain and Germany.

One of the main tourist attractions in Aalborg is Jens Bang's Stonehouse. It has often been called the "biggest and best preserved Renaissance house in the Scandinavian countries". Bang built the house in 1624. Today it houses the Swan Pharmacy. Beneath the structure is a wine cellar now open to the public. During World War II this wine cellar was the clandestine meeting place of an underground group who called themselves the Churchill Club. This group held meetings there intermittingly for years and planned various underground activities to help the cause of the Allies.

A few miles south of Aalborg is the Rebild Park. The land for this park was purchased by some Danish-Americans in 1911. Every year on the Fourth of July tens of thousands of Danes and Danish-Americans gather here to celebrate America's Independence Day. The King often takes part in the ceremony. The Stars and Stripes fly in this park on equal terms with the *Dannebrog.* There is a Lincoln Memorial Cabin, built of logs from each of the then forty-eight states of the United States. The log cabin houses mementos of Danish migration to the United States.

Old Copenhagen Canals at Wintertime with the
Thorvaldsen Museum in the Background
by
Børge Pramvig

1952

Denmark's greatest sculptor, Bertel Thorvaldsen, was born in Copenhagen in 1770. He learned the art of carving very early in life from his father, an Icelander woodcarver. At the age of eleven he enrolled in the Copenhagen Art School and his outstanding talent was soon noted. When he was twenty-six he won a scholarship to Rome where he worked for the next forty-two years. Thorvaldsen became known as the greatest sculptor of his day, and his clientele included kings and cardinals from most of the European countries.

When Thorvaldsen was sixty-eight, the Danish Government prevailed upon him to return to Copenhagen and make it his permanent home. Returning on September 17, 1838, he was given a gala welcome such as no Danish hero had ever before received. Bands were playing, the ships in the harbor were decorated with flags, flowers were showered at him from windows above, and his carriage was pulled by persons who vied for the honor. All Denmark honored him as the nation's most distinguished citizen and continued to do so until his death in 1844.

Thorvaldsen willed the City of Copenhagen his sculptures, art collections and fortune. The Thorvaldsen Museum, built to house this collection, was opened to the public in 1848. The great sculptor is buried in the courtyard and, like the Emporer Napoleon, is one of the world's few noted men to have a building surrounding his grave.

The museum is a simple building of yellow stucco and is unique in its external frieze depicting Thorvaldsen's return to Copenhagen. Inside the museum can be found all Thorvaldsen's works, either the originals or castings.

Boat of His Majesty, the King of Denmark,
in Greenland Waters
by
Kjeld Bonfils

1953

This was the centennial year for Bing & Grøndahl and an important year in the history of Greenland. Greenland had been considered a crown colony of Denmark since 1721 when Hans Egede, the Danish missionary, established a colony at Godthaab. The Constitution Act of 1953 gave to Greenland the status of a part of the Danish Realm, sharing equal rights with Denmark. This Act made other important changes in the Danish government. It abolished the Upper House of Parliament, leaving the country with only one governing body. It also provided that a woman could inherit the throne, paving the way for Princess *Margrethe* (Margaret) to someday succeed her father and become Queen Margaret II.

The Constitution Act of 1953 allows Greenland to elect two members to sit with the other 177 in the *Folketing* (Danish Parliament). Matters concerning Greenland are handled by a Minister for Greenland. Matters of local concern are taken up jointly by a Danish official, the Commissioner, and a locally elected Council.

This Christmas Plate commemorates a visit of King Frederik IX and Queen Ingrid to Greenland. It was the second time in history that the Greenlanders had been so honored by their king. When the royal yacht *Dannebrog* docked at Godthaab, Greenland's largest town (present population, 2700), all the people turned out and gave their traditional nine cheers. The *Dannebrog* is shown in the icy waters of Davis Strait just off the rockbound coast of Greenland. Much of Greenland is made up of one of the wildest and most desolate mountain regions of the world.

Birthplace of Hans Christian Andersen
by
Børge Pramvig

1954

Hans Christian Andersen, Denmark's great writer of fairy tales, was born in Odense on the island of Funen April 2, 1805. He was the only child of a poor shoemaker. During his early years the family lived and worked in one room. His father died when he was eleven, and two years later his mother was remarried to a man who had little interest in the boy. His mother wanted him to become a tailor, but he had always dreamed of becoming a famous actor.

At the age of fourteen he went to Copenhagen and for several years tried to find a place on the Danish stage, either as an actor or a singer. After repeated failures and much heartbreak, Andersen decided to try for a literary career. Having had little formal education, it was necessary for him to return to school for several years. He wrote constantly – poems, plays, novels, fairy tales and eventually an autobiography. After several years Andersen's literary works became recognized in many countries of the world. He traveled extensively throughout Europe and was friend to many of the great personalities of the day. Although he remained a bachelor for all his seventy years, it was not of his own choosing. Andersen was known to have been in love with at least three women, the most famous of whom was Jenny Lind, but none returned his love. He always thought of himself as a poet, dramatist and novelist, but the world remembers Andersen today as a writer of fairy tales.

The birthplace of Hans Christian Andersen was opened as a museum in 1908, but in 1930 had to be enlarged with additional buildings. In the museum may be found the letters, manuscripts, pictures and personal belongings of the author. There is also a library of about 2500 editions of his works in about forty-five different languages.

The Kalundborg Church
by
Kjeld Bonfils

1955

Kalundborg is a small town on the western coast of Zealand. The town has colorful streets, a picturesque market square, a railhead, and a port navigable all year.

The unique brick church is the main point of interest in Kalundborg. As were many of the old Danish churches, the Kalundborg Church was originally built to be used as a fortress as well as a place of worship. It was built in 1170 by Esbern Snare, twin brother of Bishop Absalon, founder of Copenhagen. The church is constructed in the form of a Greek Cross, and is unique in that it has one rectangular and four octagonal towers surmounted by spires. There is an octagonal tower over each of the four wings. These are dedicated to the saints, Anne, Gertrude, Catherine, and Mary Magdalene. The fifth and highest tower is rectangular and rises in the center of the cross. It was necessary to rebuild the center tower in 1871 after the original collapsed. This tower is dedicated to Our Lady. Inside the church is a carved wooden reredos dating back to 1650 and a notable granite font. The churchyard is enclosed by an old brick wall.

The church stands on a hill and the five clustered towers pointing heavenward are impressive at quite a distance. One of the most picturesque views is from the ferry that runs between Kalundborg and Aarhus in Jutland.

In the vicinity of the church are a number of medieval buildings including some of the oldest in the country. A little west of the church is a park in which the ruins of the Kalundborg Castle may be seen.

Christmas in Copenhagen
by
Kjeld Bonfils

1956

Christmas time in Denmark is very much as it is in other lands. It is a time for family festivity, for being good neighbors, for renewing friendships, and for helping those less fortunate. There is always an excitement about the season, part of which is undoubtedly genuine and part of which has been brought about by the commercialization of the holiday.

This Christmas Plate shows how the streets of Copenhagen are decorated for the Christmas season with garlands, colored lights, bells and stars. All the shops decorate for Christmas, and each has its own Christmas tree. Always, too, there is the big tree in the Town Hall Square (shown on the 1930 plate), twinkling with a myriad of lights. Copenhagen is lovely to behold at this season of the year.

On the last two Sundays before Christmas, the shops in the main part of Copenhagen open at four o'clock in the afternoon. Long before they open, though, the streets are teeming with people who come not only to shop, but also to greet friends. The music of at least one band can often be heard, adding to the festive spirit of the occasion. The people fill not only the sidewalks but the street as well. For this reason it is necessary to close off the main streets to traffic, and the buses and cars must creep as best they can through side streets and alleys. Even though the wind may be blowing and the temperature very low, the crowds move along at a pace that would suggest a warm summer evening.

A trip to the heart of Copenhagen on one of these last two Sunday afternoons before Christmas is definitely part of celebrating the Yule in the capital city of Denmark.

Christmas Candles
by
Kjeld Bonfils

1957

Hans Christian Andersen in his beloved tale *The Fir Tree* tells how the tree is selected in the woods and then brought into the home where it is decorated with little nets, hearts, and cones filled with sweets. There are also gilded apples and walnuts hanging from its branches! There are garlands of tinsel, flags, candles and everything! "Was I really born to such glorious destiny?", the fir tree wondered.

The hearts and cones have been cut out of colored paper and pasted or woven together by the children of the family during cozy December evenings. No one seems to know why there must be hearts and cones on the tree, other than that there always have been. The candles are always real candles, never electric. This may sound dangerous to Americans who burn the electric lights on their trees sometimes for weeks before and after Christmas Day. The candles of the Danish Christmas tree burn only on Christmas Eve, and then are closely watched. Although the Danish people seldom use candles in their windows at Christmas, they do use a lot of them in decorating. The Danes refer to them as "living light" as they flicker softly in bowls, often with fir cones and pussy willow around the base.

The people of Denmark do place lighted candles in their windows one night of the year. When the Danes heard of their liberation on May 4, 1945, almost every home hit upon the idea of putting a lighted candle in the window. At the time it was a spontaneous gesture, but since that time it has become the custom to place a lighted candle in the window on the evening of May 4 to show the world that the light of freedom is still glowing in Denmark.

Santa Claus
by
Kjeld Bonfils

1958

It is not unusual for a member of the family or a family friend to dress up as Santa Claus or his more customary Danish counterpart, *Jule-nissen* (see story for 1959 plate). Here is shown a little girl answering a knock on the door on Christmas Eve to find Santa Claus with a bag of toys over one shoulder and the Danish flag over the other. Santa joins the family group and gives gifts to all the children.

A quaint old custom of Denmark is practiced by the young people on New Year's Eve. Throughout the year each household saves its broken crockery, and when it becomes dark the young people smash the cracked and broken dishes against the front doors of their favorite friends. Then they run, but not very far or very fast because it is part of the game that, if caught, they are invited in for hot doughnuts. The citizen with the most broken crockery before his door on New Year's Day is the most beloved citizen of the community.

The Rønnebaek Church, located near Naestved in Southern Zealand, is shown on the right of this plate. This is a typical village church from the Middle Ages and possibly was consecrated to St. Benedict. On the church door are four iron figures resembling horseshoes. The old people in the village tell a legend that the horseshoes belonged to a live horse that was once immured under the porch. They claim that when the plague raged a ghost-horse came running through the streets of Rønnebaek and the surrounding countryside shouting, "Get out! Get out!" One farmer, placing himself in his doorway, cried to the ghost-horse, "Pass by my home, please!" This home is said to have been the only one not touched by the plague.

146

Christmas Eve
by
Kjeld Bonfils

1959

While the 1958 Christmas Plate shows Santa Claus who has gained a degree of popularity in Denmark in recent years, this plate shows the Danish *Jule-nissen*, a popular character for many generations. Here *Jule-nissen* is shown as he dances around the Christmas tree with the family. He is similar to Santa Claus because he always brings gifts for everyone, and like an Irish leprechaun in that he is normally thought of as an elf that is around the house all during the year keeping an eye on everyone and seeing that everything goes smoothly. The *nissen* normally lives in the attic of the house, but somehow the children are never able to see him there. It is appropriate that the family cat is shown on the same plate as the *nissen* because they are good friends. Always on Christmas Eve the children place a bowl of rice and milk in the attic for the *nissen*. The bowl is licked clean on Christmas morning, and the family cat is then usually found purring in a corner of the attic.

Cats are now popular with many people in Denmark but their history does not go very far back in that country. They were first introduced there during the Middle Ages as presents from Oriental potentates. The prevalent race is the short-haired cat which originated from Persian ancestors. Siamese cats are also popular as they make intelligent and sensitive pets.

The first history of cats goes back to Egypt about 2500 B.C. They were often revered and shown great honors. In the Roman Empire cats were protected by law and when one was sent abroad as a present it was given a name which was entered in a register.

148

Danish Village Church
by
Kjeld Bonfils

O

1960

Østerlars Church is one of seven round churches still found in Denmark today. It is the largest and perhaps the most interesting of the four round churches on the island of Bornholm. These churches were built in the thirteenth century and were designed to be places of refuge as well as worship. The first floor was used as a place of worship while the second and third floors were outright fortresses. There was obviously a definite plan in the location of the four Bornholm churches as they are separated by approximately the same distance and all are situated inland. They were planned as a network of fortified churches that could be used as strongholds should the island be invaded.

Bornholm is located in the Baltic Sea between Denmark and Sweden. During the time of the building of the round churches, the inhabitants had much to fear from the Wendish pirates who roamed this area.

Around the upper part of this church are various religious paintings dating back to 1230. They start with one of the Nativity Scene and end with one of the Last Judgment. In this latter scene the artist, in an effort to indicate ecclesiastical rank beyond question, used the size of a man's protruding stomach as a measure of his importance. The lower priests are shown as lean, gaunt fellows, while the more important ones are given a more ample central bulge. The bishops were given monstrous paunches. To those living in that day this told the story plainly and no one would have thought of laughing.

The building to the left of the round church is the belfry which was built several years after the church.

Winter Harmony
by
Kjeld Bonfils

1961

An old nursery rhyme is supposed to have inspired the artist to paint the scene shown on this Christmas Plate. Although the poet is unknown, it is believed that the poem originated in Sweden. It has been set to music and for a long time has been a Danish folk song. The nursery rhyme is as follows:

Danish	*English translation*
Lille egern sad	*Tiny squirrel sat*
paa sin gren saa glad	*So happily on her bench*
pudsed' snuden sin	*Blowing her nose*
med sin lab saa fin,	*With her paw so fine*
dens smaa unger tre	*While her three little young ones*
havde ly og lae	*Found shelter*
i det store gamle fyrretrae.	*In the big old pine.*

The plate shows the red squirrel, the most common squirrel of Denmark, sitting on the branch of a pine tree, nibbling on a pine cone. This squirrel has long red ears and is a different species than the red squirrel found in the United States. Its Latin name is *sciurus vulgaris.* Although it is a beautiful animal it is being killed in some localities because it does great harm to trees and birds. The number of this squirrel is difficult to control, however, as the species multiplies quite rapidly.

The church seen in the background is the white and red Kundby Church. This church can be seen at a great distance as it is situated on a hill surrounded by open fields. Kundby is about seven miles west of the city of Holbaek on the island of Zealand.

152

Winter Night
by
Kjeld Bonfils

1962

Archaeologists have established that man has lived in Denmark for at least six thousand years and possibly for as long as ten thousand years. It is known that a highly developed chieftain culture existed several thousand years ago in this area. The many cairns found scattered throughout the country are ancient monuments marking burial places of chieftains of various tribes. This plate illustrates a cairn at Mols in East Jutland.

The first agriculture in this area dates from about 2500 B.C. Denmark, being the warmest of the Scandinavian countries due to the influence of the Gulf Stream, probably supported the largest number of tribesmen in the early years. At any rate, there have been more archaeological discoveries made in Denmark than in the other northern countries.

During the Stone Age (3000-1800 B.C.) Denmark's abundance of flint and lack of metals resulted in a highly developed technique of flint-cutting. Many relics of the Bronze Age (1800-500 B.C.) show that the people were quite advanced in the making of bronze implements, costume jewelry, et cetera. The Iron Age came next and extended to about A.D. 800 when the Viking Age commenced. It was probably during the Iron Age that the people started believing in the old Nordic gods – Odin, Thor and Frey.

One of the two famous Jelling Stones (runic stones found in East Jutland) was erected by Harald Bluetooth (940-985) and on it is written that Bluetooth was "the Harald who won all Denmark and Norway and made the Danes Christian". The inscription was an exaggeration, but Harald Bluetooth did start the nation toward Christianity. The stone bears in relief a picture of Christ on the Cross.

The Christmas Elf
by
Henry Thelander

1963

The ever-popular Danish Christmas elf *Jule-nissen* is imaginatively portrayed on this plate as he exists in the minds of Danish children. Although *Jule-nissen* lives in the farmhouse invisibly, the children know that he is always somewhere near and is dressed in gray, except for his gay red nightcap. All during the year he takes a special interest in the livestock and household pets. He keeps them quiet and sees that they are fed and bedded properly. He also looks after the welfare of the family and brings gifts to the children at Christmas.

Jacob Riis, the Danish-American who was one of the first important social workers in America and whom Theodore Roosevelt once declared "The most useful citizen of the United States in his time", told about his childhood days in Denmark in his book *The Old Town*. When writing about *Jule-nissen,* he related: *"When I was a boy we never sat down to our Christmas Eve dinner until a bowl of rice and milk had been taken up to the attic, where he lived with the martin and its young, and kept an eye upon the house – saw that everything ran smoothly. I never met him myself, but I know the house cat must have done so. No doubt they were well acquainted; for when in the morning I went in for the bowl, there it was, quite dry and licked clean, and the cat purring in the corner. So, being there all night, she must have seen and likely talked with him."*

This plate shows a farmer's wife bringing to *Jule-nissen* and his friend, the cat, a generous serving of *risengrod* (rice pudding) to which has probably been added an extra lump of butter. It is believed that the family can be assured true Christmas happiness only after the Yule treat has been placed in the attic for the little elf.

The Fir Tree and The Hare
by
Henry Thelander

1964

Hans Christian Andersen's story entitled *The Fir Tree* has provided the inspiration for the enchanting scene on this year's plate.

The little fir tree was quite unhappy because of its small size. It looked with envy at the tall, majestic trees nearby. For two winters the hare was able to jump right over the top of the little tree. The third winter, though, the fir had grown so tall that the hare was forced to hop around it. Yet the tree was not happy for long! It wanted to be chosen by the woodsmen who came each year to cut down the tallest and straightest trees to be used as masts on stately ships that sailed the seven seas. How the little fir longed for such an adventurous life!

Near Christmas time each year other men came into the woods looking for the more shapely of the smaller trees. The sparrow told the fir that these trees were taken to the city and elaborately decorated. The little tree thought this, too, might be an exciting adventure.

Finally there came a Christmas when the little tree was the first to be felled. Soon thereafter it found itself standing in the center of a large room, surrounded by happy people, and decorated so magnificently that it trembled at the thought of so much splendor. The tree felt that this truly would be a glorious life but, alas, the next day it was stripped of its decorations and taken to the attic. In the early Spring it was dragged down the stairs. "Now" thought the little fir, "surely I shall see my old friends again – the birds, the hare, the other trees and the sunshine!" Such was not to be its fate, however! It was cut into small pieces and burned, and as the tree burned, it seemed to make little crackling noises. These were really moans, because as Andersen said, "The tree knew that it was all over, and the story's over as well! All, all over! And that's the way of every story!"

Bringing Home the Christmas Tree
by
Henry Thelander

4

1965

The place is Rebild Park in Rold Woods. The time is the Sunday before Christmas, and the forest is a shimmering wonderland of snow. A watchful doe and fawn stand immobile as a happy, but weary, family pass near them. This family has been in search of the most beautiful tree of all, to be used as a Christmas tree. It is now late in the day and they are going home, dragging their freshly-cut tree over the snow. A Christmas-like star twinkles brightly overhead, in a sense smiling down at the tranquil scene.

The trees that may be felled in this forest are marked in advance. Each year on the Sunday before Christmas, families are permitted to come and cut down their own *Jul* trees, paying for them as they leave the park. The excursion into the forest to select a tree is ofttimes one of the highlights of the Christmas season.

It rightfully has been said that Rebild Park is unique among international monuments to peace. It is the only park in the world that has been established specifically to celebrate the American Independence Day, July 4th. (See story for 1951 plate.) The park, originally 200 acres but now covering 425 acres of rolling hills, is always open to the public. On the Fourth of July both the American and Danish flags fly from every hilltop. The fifty state flags of the United States also are displayed in the park at this time. Tens of thousands of Danish-Americans rendezvous here on this special day. Many come for the entire day to enjoy the rustic beauty of the park as well as the program for the occasion, which always includes speeches by prominent Danish and American citizens.

160

Home for Christmas
by
Henry Thelander

6

1966

For untold centuries Danish fishermen have braved the North Sea for a livelihood. Often referred to as the "Mariner's Graveyard," there are few seas among those sailed extensively that are more rough than the North Sea. Because of the relatively shallow depth, steep and confused waves can develop in a short time. Nowadays all ships, except the very smallest, are equipped with radio and the fishermen can get weather reports several times a day. At the first mention of a possible gale, preparations are made to seek the nearest harbor. Perhaps equally feared in the North Sea is fog, which occurs frequently.

Although many of the fishing boats of Denmark today are very large ones capable of staying out weeks at a time, the ones shown on this plate are of the smaller type, usually handled by two to four men. On the bow of each ship are two letters which identify the port from which it hails, and several numbers which have been assigned to that particular vessel.

On this year's plate the boats are returning home to one of the harbors on the west side of Jutland, the peninsular region of Denmark. It is Christmas Eve and they are following the old Danish custom of having a small spruce tree at the masthead. Perhaps the fishermen are returning early so they may go with their families to the Christmas Eve church service. The lights on the ships have been turned on as the days around Christmas are quite short, particularly in northern Jutland. It is obvious, too, that the sea has been rough as they made their way homeward for the stabilizing sails have been hoisted. As they enter the harbor, however, the men are thinking not of the rough sea behind them, but of the forthcoming holiday festivities with their loved ones.

162

Sharing the Joy of Christmas
by
Henry Thelander

1967

On this year's plate, Henry Thelander again has exemplified the spirit of Christmas by portraying a little boy feeding the birds on Christmas Eve. The little lad will be called Jens, a typical Danish name.

During the long evenings of the previous summer Jens helped his father build the bird feeder from native woods around their home. It was placed among the small fir trees in their garden where the family could enjoy watching the several species of birds common to that area.

The feeder has been in place for several months, and the birds have learned that always food can be found there. Now it is Christmas Eve and a blanket of snow covers the countryside, but Jens, bundled up in his heavy coat, does not feel the cold as he gives a Christmas treat to the birds. It is an old tradition in Denmark that the birds and domestic animals share the joy of Christmas by receiving special rations.

After feeding the birds, Jens will take a bowl of rice pudding, prepared by his mother, up to the attic and leave it there for *Jul-nissen*, the Danish Christmas elf. This is the Danish equivalent of the American custom of the child setting out a treat for Santa Claus on Christmas Eve.

Jens must not tarry as the hour is drawing near when he will go to church with the family to participate in the five o'clock Christmas Eve worship service. When they return home, there will be the big Christmas dinner, and then the dance around the tree, and last but not least, all the presents!

As he feeds the birds, surely Jens is thinking that this is the best day in the whole year!

Christmas in Church
by
Henry Thelander

1968

In Denmark all who possibly can, stop working the day before Christmas until after New Year's Day. The normal salutation upon meeting friends during this season is "May God bless your Christmas; may it last till Easter!"

The 1968 plate depicts a highlight of the Christmas season – the 5 o'clock church service on Christmas Eve. The churches are beautifully decorated with evergreens and are lighted with dozens of candles.

A model of a sailing vessel may be found hanging from the ceiling in many of the Danish churches. The sea always has played an important part in the lives of the Danish people. Before Christianity spread to this area, the Vikings worshipped many gods, including Ran, their sea-goddess. Sometimes they called the sea "the land of Ran." It was believed that Ran had a giant net into which she drew down to her domain those lost at sea. Before important sea voyages and other warlike expeditions, human beings were offered as sacrifices to the gods.

Christianity came slowly to this northland as these people found it difficult to give up the gods they had believed in for centuries. Harald Klak claimed in 826 A.D. to have converted the Danes to Christianity, but actually it was another hundred years or more before Christianity gained much of a foothold. When it did, the people gave up belief in their old gods, and many of the old customs disappeared. The sea still provided a livelihood for many of these people. It is not surprising then that the early Christians started the custom of hanging ship models in their churches. They were expressing the hope that their new God would bless their ships and the men who sailed upon them.

166

Arrival of Christmas Guests
by
Henry Thelander

1969

The Christmas Eve scene on this plate could take place this year, or it could have been drawn from a similar setting a century or more ago. The Danish people readily accept new ideas when progress is the result, but even then they like to hold on to what was good of the old traditions.

Portrayed is the hostess of a country home as she comes forward to greet her guests, some relatives who have come by horse-drawn sleigh to share the festivities of Christmas Eve.

The woman coming from the barn with two pails of milk, followed by the family cat, would indicate the milking is finished, and undoubtedly the other farm chores of the evening have been completed. After the horse has been unhitched from the sleigh, taken to the barn and given his Christmas meal, the family and guests will walk to the village church, situated a short distance from the rear of the house. All will return after the Christmas Eve service to partake of the Christmas feast, which is followed by carol singing and the gift exchange.

The farmstead is of the half timber design which still can be seen in much of the Danish countryside. Under the snow is probably a thatched roof. Not only do the Danes believe the thatched roof to be picturesque, but many contend that it is still the best roof, providing better insulation than the tile type more commonly used now. The cost today, as well as the fire hazard involved, usually prohibits the use of thatched roofs in new construction. Many farmers and householders in small towns, though, continue to keep in repair the thatched roofs they have had for many years.

Pheasants in the Snow at Christmas
by
Henry Thelander

1970

Fortunate indeed is the Danish farm family who can look out the window on Christmas Eve and see a group of ring-neck pheasants such as depicted on this year's plate. The handsome cock pheasant in the foreground adds color to the white countryside with his brilliant plumage which often grows to a length of three feet. The hen pheasants are a mottled brown, and not nearly as colorful as their male counterpart.

A native of China, the ring-neck pheasant was introduced in Europe late in the eighteenth century. They spread quickly, and today can be found in most of the northern countries. In Denmark they are considered a game bird, and the annual hunting season is during the latter part of the year. The birds will try to hide from the hunter, but when flushed, they can rise almost vertically at great speed. They can maintain this speed, however, only for short distances.

Pheasants eat seeds and tender plants as well as many injurious insects. In the wintertime when food is hard to find, they sometimes can be seen sharing the fare of the farmer's chickens.

The ring-neck pheasant is one of America's favorite game birds. It was introduced here much later than in Europe. In 1881, Judge O. N. Denny, our Consul General in Shanghai, China, sent thirty of these birds to Oregon. Twenty-six survived and were released in the Willamette Valley where they multiplied rapidly. In 1887 Rutherford Stuyvesant brought a number of pheasants from England to his New Jersey estate. Today they are found in all the northern states and fairly far south in the western part of the country.

Christmas at Home
by
Henry Thelander

1971

The time is Christmas Eve. After attending the five o'clock church service, the family has returned home and partaken of the Christmas feast. This is the time the children have eagerly awaited. Mother is holding the Baby as she plays the old Christmas songs on the piano. Father, Daughter, Grandmother and Grandfather sing and dance around the gaily decorated tree. Peace, harmony and happiness obviously reign in this home on this holy night.

The family is singing old Danish Christmas songs. One hymn they always sing is *"Stille Nat"* ("Silent Night"). "Merry Christmas, Lovely Christmas" to the tune of "Holy Night" is also a favorite. After the singing comes the gift exchange. In some homes *Julenissen* or Santa Claus joins the family circle and distributes the gifts.

Christmas in Denmark, as it is in all Christendom, is a time for bringing the family together. Here all the festivities take place on Christmas Eve. Christmas Day is normally spent more quietly, giving the adults an opportunity to relax and visit with each other, and the children a chance to play with their new toys. Mother and Grandmother often get together before Christmas to bake the many tempting goodies enjoyed during this holiday season. Mother and Father have spent long December evenings with the children making many of the ornaments for the tree. The typical Danish tree is decorated with real candles, lighted only on Christmas Eve, and is topped with a shining star.

172

Christmas in Greenland
by
Henry Thelander

1972

It is Christmas Eve in a little village in Greenland. Darkness has fallen, but it is not necessarily late. Since the northern part of the island lies north of the Arctic Circle, there are periods when the sun does not rise above the horizon, and others when it does not drop below it. The "Arctic night" lasts for four months at Thule and for about six weeks at Disko Bay. Certainly in all of Greenland the nights are long around Christmas time.

Two of the villagers are returning home, hurrying because it is very cold and also they want to get home before the Christmas festivities begin. Perhaps they are returning from a larger settlement where they were able to load the sledge with many things that will bring joy to the villagers during the holiday season. Even the sledge dogs are happy to see the lights in the distance.

Greenland was considered by most to be a far-off Arctic territory before World War II. During the war air bases were established there and today airlines use these airfields as refueling stops, thereby giving people an opportunity, not formerly possible, of getting a glimpse of this northern land.

The original population of Greenland was Eskimo, but since 1721 many Danes have settled there and introduced many of their customs to the island. Christmas in Greenland undoubtedly is very much like Christmas in Denmark, except for the isolation of the villages. Most habitation is along the seacoast and, during the winter when the water is frozen, dog teams represent the primary mode of transportation.

Country Christmas
by
Henry Thelander

175

1973

Henry Thelander's theme for this plate will take many back to their childhood days when they went to a large country home on Christmas Eve for the yearly celebration with grandparents, aunts, uncles, cousins and other seldom seen members of the family. For the grownups it was an opportunity to catch up on the family news for the past year and for the children, a time of excitement and anticipation.

The half-timber house pictured, a combination of wood and masonry, is typical of many Danish country homes. These homes are so well built and well cared for that it is difficult to tell whether they are a few years or a few hundred years old. In many cases several generations of a family have grown up in the same house. Homes built in Denmark seem to stand much longer than homes generally are expected to last in America. Banks often give as much as a sixty year mortgage on a house in Denmark which is unheard-of in this country.

The home on this plate is ablaze with light and undoubtedly is festively decorated inside. Even the fir tree in front of the house has been brightly lighted, indicating to the passersby that this home is happy that Christmas Eve has come again. Mother and Daughter are already being greeted at the door while Father and Son follow through the gate with their arms full of Christmas gifts. All have eagerly awaited this special night of the year. Young and old alike are pleased that there has been a recent snowfall. Snow always gives the countryside a more picturesque appearance and most will agree adds much to the enjoyment of the holiday season.

Christmas in the Village
by
Henry Thelander

1974

It is Christmas Eve in a little Danish village. Once again the time has come for the men to close the shops early, for the women to put aside preparations for the Christmas dinner, and for the children to temporarily forget the gifts they hope to receive later in the evening. Now is the long awaited hour when all–young and old –go together to the village church for the annual Christmas Eve service. The evening is obviously cold as the lake is frozen over except for a small area.

Two graceful swans are featured in the foreground of the scene on this plate. Henry Thelander has chosen to portray the mute swan, one of Denmark's favorite waterfowl. Although usually silent, this swan can produce a twangy trumpeting note and will hiss or snort when annoyed. The legendary belief that this swan sings a beautiful song just before it dies is the origin of the expression "swan song".

The male swan, known as the cob, is a very large bird weighing up to twenty pounds or more and measuring as much as five feet from beak to tail. The pen (female) is a little smaller. The same pair generally stays together for life unless something happens to one. The cob brings materials from which the pen builds a huge nest. Both incubate the three to ten large pale green eggs, the cob mainly at night. The cygnets hatch in about five weeks and in four months are fully fledged. They usually remain with their parents through the Winter, but are chased away by the old cob in the Spring. Swans add much enjoyment to the long Danish Winter for the household fortunate enough to have them near by.

Christmas at the Old Water Mill
by
Henry Thelander

1975

Scattered throughout Denmark can be found many charming old water mills such as Kjelddals Mill in Jutland which appears on this year's plate. This mill was saved from extinction in 1966 by the Danish National Museum Mill Preservation Board.

At one time as many as 3000 water mills could be found in Denmark but today there are only about fifty left. The history of water mills in Denmark goes back for many centuries. Quite a few were built during the reign of the Valdemar kings (1157-1182) as it was then considered wasteful to let the water run into the sea without utilizing its power for the grinding of grain.

Some of the water mills built in the Middle Ages were in all probability built by monks coming from England. This is indicated by such names as *Klostermølle* (Convent Mill) and *Munkemølle* (Friar's Mill).

In the 17th and 18th centuries the millering trade became so monopolized that not only were small farmhouse mills outlawed, but even hand querns were not permitted. This monopoly existed until 1862.

For his pay the miller was supposed to retain only one-eighth of all grain brought in, from which he in turn paid his dues to the Squire, the Crown or the Church. These dues were always paid on St. Martimas Day, the day set aside to honor the patron saint of the miller. It seems that there may have been times when there was some doubt in the customers' minds as to the accuracy of the method used to measure the grain. There was also a rumor that perhaps the miller did not use all his grain to make flour. In any event there was an old saying that "A miller is never so drunk that he forgets to take his full quota."

Christmas Welcome
by
Henry Thelander

"Look, Mother, Daddy is here!" the little girl shouts to her mother as she runs to greet her father who has just arrived. Her father, like all Danish fishermen, has been hurrying home to join his family for the biggest celebration of the year — Christmas.

The church in the background is typical of the many Danish village churches built some 800 years ago in the Gothic style. They were usually surrounded by half-timber houses, many of which may still be seen throughout the country.

The scene represents one of the many fishing villages on the island of Zealand, where also the city of Copenhagen, the capitol, is situated.

The island of Zealand boasts quite an interesting origin. Legend has it that Gefion, the Nordic Goddess of fecundity, married the Swedish King Gylfe. She bore him four sons, and when they had all come of age, she decided she wanted to settle in Denmark. She then asked the King not only for a divorce but also for some land on which to build a new home. The King granted her the divorce but only as much land as her four sons could plow away within twenty-four hours. Gefion, mastering witchcraft, transformed her four sons into bullocks, who plowed away from Sweden within the time limit what is now the island of Zealand. It is alleged that the land taken from Sweden left a gap now filled by Lake Vanern, which is approximately the same size and shape as Zealand.

The legend has been immortalized by the Danish sculptor, Anders Bundgaard, who in 1918 created the imposing Gefion Fountain at the approach to the park at *Langelinie* in Copenhagen. This fountain depicts the famous plowing scene with the four bullocks straining at the plow as Gefion, right arm raised with lash, urges the beasts to even greater effort.

Copenhagen Christmas
by
Henry Thelander

Christmas night in starlit Copenhagen! What a wonderful view to behold! *Julenissen,* dressed as usual in gray with a red cap, looks out from the skylight of his attic home and sees the illuminated Christmas tree in an adjacent dwelling. The ever-popular Christmas elf knows that this is the night he will receive his customary Christmas treat. A bowl filled to the brim with *risengrod* (rice pudding) and milk will be placed in the attic for him to enjoy together with his close pal, the family cat. According to legend *Julenissen* will, in return, not only whisper into the ear of Santa the list of Christmas gifts for the children but will also assure the happiness of the family for another year.

We are in old downtown Copenhagen with its popular landmark, the Round Tower. This lofty building was constructed as an observatory for the nearby University while serving at the same time as a tower for the adjoining Trinity Church. Designed by architect Hans van Steenwinckel, Junior, the tower was built in 1637-1642 by Christian the Fourth, the famous builder among the Danish Kings. This king was so interested in leaving behind him great buildings as monuments that he often strolled through the streets of Copenhagen carrying a ruler to check how well the masons and carpenters were conforming to the architectural plans.

The 36 meter (118 feet) high Round Tower is famous for its 209 meter (685 feet) winding brick staircase. In 1716 while on a state visit to Denmark, Czar Peter the Great of Russia rode to the top of the tower on horseback, followed by his Czarina in a horse-drawn cart. Luckily they both returned unhurt from their experience and were hailed by the excited crowd for their daring.

Today walking up the winding staircase is a must for all visitors to the city. Their exertion is rewarded by a fantastic panoramic view of the more than 800 year old capitol of Denmark.

A Christmas Tale
by
Henry Thelander

The Christmas season always brings memories of past Christmases to both young and old. Many can remember sitting at Grandmother's knee listening as she read aloud her favorite Christmas stories. The grandmother on this year's plate could be reading *The Fir Tree* by Hans Christian Andersen, a story the Danes never cease to enjoy.

The scene portrayed is traditional in many lands. Only the decorations on the Christmas tree indicate that we are looking into a Danish home. The Danish people still prefer to use real candles. The decorations are handmade by the family during long December evenings. The cones and hearts have been a part of the Danish Christmas tree for generations.

The idea of a Christmas tree, as we know it, originated in Germany during the early 17th century. Some credit Martin Luther with having first introduced it, but this has not been authenticated. By the mid-19th century its popularity was well established throughout Germany and had spread to many other lands. It was introduced in Denmark about 1830.

There have been many legends regarding the origin of the Christmas tree. According to one, it all started one stormy Christmas Eve when a family living in the forest had settled around a cheerful fire. They heard a knock at the door, and upon opening it, found a little child, very cold, hungry and exhausted. He was welcomed into the household, warmed and fed. Little Hans insisted on giving up his bed to the stranger. In the morning the family was awakened by the singing of angels and they found their little guest had been transfigured into the Christ-Child. Before leaving, the Christ-Child broke off a branch from a fir tree, set it in the earth, and said, "I have gladly received your gifts, and this is My gift to you. Henceforth this tree shall always bear its fruit at Christmas and you shall always have abundance".